Ministers
Manual

Herbert L Beierle

Ministers Manual

Herbert L Beierle

for
**MINISTERS
OF
GOD UNLIMITED CHURCHES
AND METAPHYSICALLY ORIENTED CLERGY**

First Printing 1976
Second Printing 1978
Third Printing 1982
Fourth Printing 1985
Fifth Printing 1997—REVISED

COPYRIGHT © 1997 BY
UNI PRESS
Campo California 91906-3213

PRINTED IN THE UNITED STATES OF AMERICA

Also by Herbert L Beierle

Art and Science of Wholeness
Song of the Spirit
Illumination, Handbook of Ascended Masters
Autobiography of god
The Relative
The Relative/Absolute
ABSOLUTE
Practitioners Manual
Ministers Manual
A Gift from Self to Self
I Am Number One
My Inner Journey
The Weathering
Quiet, Healing Zone!
Why I Can Say I Am God
How to Give a Healing Treatment
Practice Reality
Three Hour Meditation
The Law of Cause and Effect
Inexhaustible Laughter of Heaven—BLISS

Many of these books are available in
German, Italian, French and Russian.

ISBN 0-940480-03-4

3|13

God Unlimited/University of Healing
UNI PRESS 1101 Far Valley Road
Campo, California 91906-3213, U.S.A.
Phone: (619) 478-5111 ♦ Fax: (619) 478-5013
E-Mail: unihealing@fia.net ♦ **Website:** http//www.university-of-healing

BV
552.1
345
1997

CONTENTS

Page

Our Business
Is not
Merely to be sinless,
But to be God!

Plotinus

Theme 1

PURPOSE
OF THE MANUAL

DEDICATION

• • • to the art and science of service to our fellowman at its most meaningful level.

• • • to the joy of being a living example of what we now believe.

• • • to the ultimate good of being that which we truly are—GOD!

MANUAL FOR MINISTERS AND PRACTITIONERS

*A*s metaphysical ministers and practitioners we desire to have a manual to guide us in the operation of our calling.

Many denominations and professional publishing houses have produced such manuals but somehow none have met the needs of the metaphysical minister/practitioner who diligently chooses to not only be one of the many in the field—but to be their very best!

In all of my activities of growing in consciousness I have aspired to be my personal best as a professional in my field. To that end I prepared myself.

It is in this light that I now present this manual to the ministers of the Church of God Unlimited, a church of meditation, teaching and healing, *and to every other metaphysically oriented minister and practitioner.*

Rev Herbert L Beierle, PhD, DD
Dean and Founder
God Unlimited/University of Healing
Campo California

GRATITUDE TO MY SOURCES

*W*hile most of the material in this manual is the creation of God within the author, thanks are due to the various other sources utilized for services, quotations and information.

Special appreciation goes to *Science of Mind,* by Ernest Holmes. This textbook is one of the finest efforts ever to be published in the field of metaphysics. The United Church of Religious Science for their *MINISTERS MANUAL* from which were drawn many of the services that were rewritten for GOD UNLIMITED church use. From Unity School of Christianity came many of the ideas on silence and healing groups. From Divine Science have come many healing projects. From Christian Science their infallible use of the concept of the ABSOLUTE relative to God and their healing programs. Concepts have been taken from other New Thought organizations, from Spiritualism, from Theosophy, and going back to Phineas P. Quimby and Ralph Waldo Emerson—and to the files of history to the great thinkers of all time who have blessed us with their knowledge and thought. And for the contributions from the thoughtful competence of the following monks of the Absolute Monastery: Abbot Ellen Jermini, Ilse Wenk, Ingeborg Puchert, Stefan Strässle and Sylvia Enz.

Respecting our predecessors we most certainly include appreciation to Jesus the Christ, Buddha, Zoroaster, Confucius, Lao Tze, Mohammed and many others who have brought religion to a living experience for all mankind, and whose impact upon world beingness is felt in these services and ministerial conduct reported here.   ∞

OUR OBLIGATION

*T*he metaphysical minister and practitioner of GOD UNLIMITED has the obligation to fulfill a vital universal ministry, not only to the traditional Christian faith, but eclectically, drawing from the world religions and synthesizing them into the fabric of life. This means being prepared to conduct the various duties which that involves.

At the same time, there is the further obligation to present that ministry in the terms of the religious philosophy of GOD UNLIMITED as is taught in the University of Healing. The church offices performed should be done with dignity choosing the appropriate positive wording to advance the basic principles of truth.

The services presented in this manual are suggestions only, and each minister will use his own variations. It is recommended that whenever and wherever possible the conventional form of the services be expanded to express its deeper metaphysical and spiritual meaning.

It is important to note that while the marriage ceremony may be presented in many forms, it is essential from a legal point of view, that certain factors be retained. Namely: that the man and woman separately state their willingness to wed, and that the minister pronounces them husband and wife. Another instance concerns the baptismal and christening services. The service has great meaning using water as it is done at traditional baptisms, but rose petals and other items are equally significant.

On Being Immortal covers considerations of the ascending soul moving into its new dimension. The minister says, "I shall never die, for the spirit within me is God and cannot change."

The metaphysical minister and practitioner have the opportunity to lift the consciousness of those who come to him—for guidance, prayer, treatment, religious functions and services and for spiritual healing—to a new height, a new level of awareness, and thereby unfold the native divinity within.

This is the primary and only function of any metaphysical minister and practitioner, to help himself and those who come to him, to reveal the divinity which dwells within each. Further than that, there is no purpose to be!　　　∞

THE DIVINE COMMISSION

*T*he church has the responsibility of working in the area of healing.

Healing was done by Jesus. Writing in the latter part of the Second Century Iranaeus speaks of the following works of healing as performed by Christians and done by no others: giving sight to the blind and hearing to the deaf; casting out all sorts of demons; curing the weak and lame, the paralytic, those distressed in any part of the body; remedying external accidents; frequently raising the dead.

Pagans, as well as Christians, knew of the healings which were performed on nonChristians as well as Christians, and these healings were often the means of conversion to Christianity.

At the end of the Fourth Century the 17th Canon of Hippolytus ordered the following prayer be used at the ordination of bishops and presbyters:

Grant to Him, O Lord, a mild spirit and the power to remit sins. Grant to him to loose all bonds of the iniquity of demons, to heal all diseases and quickly to bend down Satan under his feet.

The words of Jesus are specific: Then he called his twelve disciples together, and gave them power and authority over the devils, and to cure diseases. And he sent them to preach the kingdom of God, and to heal the sick.[1]

As Jesus did not separate the practitioners and the ministers, so GOD UNLIMITED unites the two into one and provides both with equal possibilities to serve, treat and heal. For a practitioner and the minister always works with those who are in need.

Those who are well need no doctor but those who are seriously sick. I came not to invite righteous men, but sinners.[2]

∞

---

1   Luke 9:1,2 [KJV]

2   Matthew 9:12,13

MINISTER'S DIVINE TASK

*M*inisters are always looking for a summary of the work set before them in their several roles: minister—friend—lover.

We need look no further. In the Bible **I Corinthians 13** the work is spelled out powerfully and richly. The words *faith, hope and charity* are the watch words here. We define these words as follows: **Faith** (humility) is fidelity to one's vows and promises. **Hope** is knowing that which may now be unseen does indeed exist. **Charity** is **love** defined as nonjudgmental, nonpossessive, beneficial, benevolent thought toward ourself and others as our creation. For *Charity* we use **Love**.

Greatest Of These Is Love

THOUGH I speak with the tongues of men and of angels, and have not love, I am become as sounding brass, or a tinkling cymbal.

And though I have the gift of prophecy, and understand all mysteries, and all knowledge; and though I have all faith, so that I could remove mountains, and have not love, I am nothing.

And though I bestow all my goods to feed *the poor*, and though I give my body to be burned, and have not love, it profiteth me nothing.

Love suffereth long, *and* is kind; love envieth not; love vaunteth not itself, is not puffed up.

Doth not behave itself unseemly, seeketh not her own, is not easily provoked, thinketh no evil;

Rejoiceth not in iniquity, but rejoiceth in the truth;

Beareth all things, believeth all things, hopeth all things, endureth all things.

Love never faileth: but whether *there be* prophecies, they shall fail; whether *there be* tongues, they shall cease; whether *there be* knowledge, it shall vanish away.

For we know in part, and we prophesy in part.

But when that which is perfect is come, then that which is in part shall be done away.

When I was a child, I spake as a child, I understood as a child, I thought as a child: but when I became a man, I put away childish things.

For now we see through a glass, darkly; but then face to face: now I know in part; but then shall I know even as also I am known.

And now abideth faith, hope, love, these three; but the greatest of these *is* love. 3

---

3   1 Corinthians 13 [KJV]

WHY RITUALS
AND CEREMONIES

*R*ituals and ceremonies outwardly symbolize an inner knowingness; an inner awareness of the spirit of truth and of our Christ Consciousness. Since we are the nature of God, we choose to express it outwardly.

In participating in rituals and ceremonies we give expression in form to our faith, our strength of conviction and our love for our creator. Be it a blissful wedding occasion or assistance at or after death to the individual and the family and friend of a graduating loved one, a joyous event, it is man's nature to articulate in words and gestures his response to this experience.

Man is a creative being and this is a form of bringing forth symbolically what we experience within the depth of our very beings—a responsive reaction. Our great teacher set us an example by the symbolic liturgy he used both in his teachings and in his preaching to the people and his disciples.   ∞

CONCEPT OF GOD AND MAN

*F*or eons mankind has conceived of God as being outside, separate from himself. This *creation of God by man* has been one that he has never quite comprehended and even less used. For this reason mankind has prayed to one who was outside of himself for help and has, of course, only received this *help* sporadically, if at all.

We have come to a new vision of the creative cause of the universe and the principle behind all that exists. This new thought teaches us of a concept of beingness, rather than beingness itself. For when one thinks of a being, one has the *view* of a specific conception of a form with dimensions and a place in which it dwells.

In our wiser moments, we realize that this is not only improbable for an omnipresent creative force, but totally impossible from even our *limited* appreciation of an infinite *being*. For if whatever it is that maintains and placed all into existence is at once everywhere present, it could not be a *man on a cloud* as a specific form and manifestation—it must be universal.

Thus we dispose of one myth of God-man—or have we?

God is in all of its creation as a perfect unwritten number, everywhere at once, across time and space. Yet to realize this still more, in the infinite pattern of things there is no space or time, all is in the NOW. So one could say that in the now the infinite is in the all.

And since God is omnipresent, it is in all of its creation equally and totally. For how could God be not present at any one point. The whole must be totally complete everywhere and at all of its points of contact with any of its beingness wherever it may be extant.

From these points of view the infinite could not be less present at any point of its beingness than it is at any other point of contact with the creation of its infinite scope.

From this reasoning we could then assume that God in its absolute beingness is present everywhere, in everything, in the totality of its intelligence, knowingness, selfknowingness, substance, power and allness.

This would mean that all of the creation of the infinite would be precisely and exactly of equal ability to be, to know and to do as it is!

This would guide us to conclude that all of "existence" including man, animals, lower forms of life, plants, trees, flowers, minerals and all forms of sentient and nonsentient life have unity with the creative spirit and unity of all life, one with any other creation of the one principle.

But each of the creation has within it all of the creator.

So the conclusion to be arrived at from this type of thinking is that there is no God outside of man himself, outside of any of its own creation, that God for any of its creation is totally within its creation and can be found within at all times and especially when the creation is seeking to communicate with its creative cause.

God has now symbolically come down from the cloud.

For to pray to God in anything other than ourselves is to go around the world to reach our hand connected to our body.

As we develop the habit and awareness that we shall find all of God within our very own being we come to a rather unique position in thought saying: I AM GOD! [4]

---

[4]   Bhagavad Gita and WHY I CAN SAY I AM GOD

This is a truth that was taught to us by the great teachers throughout all time. Each said continuously:

- *KNOW THYSELF* [5]

- *Ye are gods* [6]

- *The kingdom of God is within you* [7]

- *Be ye therefore perfect, even as your Father which is in heaven is perfect* [8]

- *The kingdom of Heaven is within man* [9]

- *You are all of god right now* [10]

and so much more.

To communicate with God within means that we become still to all outer stimuli and listen to the quiet voice of the infinite as it speaks to us and tells us how to achieve the desires of our heart.

While listening we must be alert to the word that is revealed to us. It will sound just as though it were us speaking to ourselves. **For God in us sounds just like us to us**. This is where the confusion takes place so often as we seek God's desire for us in us through us. The medium of reception is the same as the medium of delivery. God speaks to us as us through us.

---

5   Socrates
6   John 10:34 [KJV]
7   Luke 17:21 [KJV]
8   Matthew 5:48 [KJV]
9   Koran
10   Egyptian Book of the Dead

This is why we must be alert to guide our listening by the idea that:

- ***The eye with which I see God is the same eye with which God sees me.*** [11]

- **IT IS GOOD FOR US, HURTS NONE AND TAKES FROM NONE!**

If it fulfills these criteria, we can be sure it is the divine within us revealing itself to us as us.

God is constantly talking to mankind.

God is constantly talking to its creation.

God is constantly revealing ITSELF to those who would listen and be alert to the beautiful constructive abundant ideas of spirit.

God, besides being omnipresent, everywhere present in all of its creation, is: omniscient and omnipotent.

This omniscience, all knowingness, is equally available to each and everyone of its creation. The ability to know "how" to do anything and all of the details concerned with carrying it out are instantly known to the inquiring mind that turns to the one source of all knowledge, God within, all will be made known to them.

The omnipotence of God, the total power of the creative force of the universe, that which brought everything into being, that which keeps the stars in their orbit—that which causes everything to be that which it is—this power is available to all of

---

11   Meister Eckart, Christian Mystic

the creation of God to use however it will—but always within man's desire.

Indeed, man can create universes too, and he does. All according to his concept of life. Man brings forth according to his belief all he desires to see in his experience. As he does it he outwardly pictures to the world about him what his concept of the universal creator is and what he believes the givingness and loving-kindness of this creative force is in his world of appearances.

This can all be changed and this can be formed out of a new cause the moment the creator desires a new experience in his world of appearances. It is not a difficult thing to do. It is merely the changing of one's thinking from limitation to abundance, from lack to fulfillment, from thinking about that which he does not want to have to that which he desires to have in his world.

So it is that the totality of God, the whole beingness of all is in each of its creation and mankind, as a creation of God, has all of these attributes available to him to use as he desires for his highest and best in his life.

All of mankind is omnipotent, omniscient and omnipresent—but each will outpicture it in his life only as he applies the principle behind it. This principle is that of conscious belief and application—conscious choice.

We believe by our recognizing anything that it is true. We apply it by speaking our word and the outward manifestation takes place for us and others.

This is a concept of God and man that works.

This is a concept of God and man that is ever revealing itself according to our use of it.

This is the greatest gift ever given, it is the gift that has been given from the very beginning of God itself to its creation NOW!

Accept!   ∞

Theme 2

MINISTER
AND
PRACTITIONER

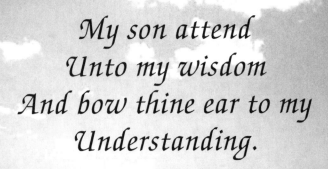

My son attend
Unto my wisdom
And bow thine ear to my
Understanding.

Proverbs 5:1 [KJV]

MINISTER/PRACTITIONER

*T*he question is often asked why GOD UNLIMITED ministers are practitioners and GOD UNLIMITED practitoners are ministers. The answer is that the work of the minister is the work of the practitioner. For a minister to place any limit upon himself in the range of his pastoral possibilities is to limit the degree to which he expresses his Godhood—and to the degree that he presumes to do that, he thus presumes to limit the power of God within himself.

A practitioner practices what he believes of the spiritual principles under which he works. A practitioner first heals himself relative to the friend and sees the friend experiencing the highest healing. The practitioner is an "agent" for the *Law of cause and effect.* As an agent/catalyst/causer, he does not become emotionally involved in the desires sought, rather the practitioner sees it done. He does not necessarily counsel people rather he does set into motion those practices which elicit the action of the Law on behalf of the friend with whom he is working. In one respect the practitioner does not advise the friend in any manner, shape or form, but primarily sets the Law in motion on their behalf toward the positive solution of their desires. *This is the highest healing.*

The minister, on the other hand, does counsel with the friend and advises in the realm of moral, social and spiritual guidance so that lives may be lived in conjunction with the end result favored. While doing this the minister views the friend from the *highest point of view* always recognizing purity and truth about him, his God given creative gift of perfection—thus bringing about the Law of cause and effect in his life to insure his recognition of this wholeness as his own and the only result of the minister-practitioner-friend relationship.

Practitioner/ministers are effective healers when healing is recognized as the friend exercising the truth about himself—returning him to the original purity and integrity born with him into all of life.

Many people who are interested in healing refrain from getting *too involved* primarily because they feel that they are the ones who must do the work. This is so far from the point! The healing minister merely recognizes the truth about the individual and by the raised state of consciousness of the minister-practitioner-friend, the healing is accomplished—the return to the original purity and integrity of the individual. It is not something that the minister/practitioner does to the person, it is what they do to their own consciousness. The minister/practitioner changes his own consciousness and may be a catalyst to the friend to change his consciousness.

The most explicit statement—found in the Bible include the words of Jesus where he commanded the disciples, and the seventy, with his great commission asking them "to observe all things whatsoever I have commanded you" [1] including healing, preaching and teaching—is: *Verily, verily, I say unto you, He that believeth on me, the* works *that I do shall he do also; and greater works than these shall he do.* [2] So the healing ministry which Jesus the Christ carried out is expected of those who would follow the teachings of the master.

All of life in this age of miracles is learning to live from our Godself. Things continually happen for which we have no rational or logical explanation. Healings take place constantly in the lives of everyone and few there are who recognize it as the working of the Law in their lives, but this is just what it is and nothing else. ∞

---

1   Matthew 28:20 [KJV]

2   John 14:12 [KJV]

THE PRACTITIONER'S ROLE

*I*t is important at the outset to clearly define the role of the practitioner of GOD UNLIMITED; his privileges, duties, obligations; his Code of Ethics; his many relationships: spiritual, ecclesiastical and personal.

The title and honor of being called *Practitioner* is earned separately but can be taken concurrently with your ministerial course for your ordination granted by GOD UNLIMITED. The *Practitioner* is licensed by GOD UNLIMITED, a church of meditation, teaching and healing.

The authority to issue each License and to govern its practice is vested in GOD UNLIMITED and given pursuant to ecclesiastical rule.

The principle function of the *Practitioner* is to practice spiritual purity and recognize: **it is done!**

The Licensed *Practitioner* is an ecclesiastical representative of the Church of God Unlimited and complies with the church role as set forth by GOD UNLIMITED.

The role of the Practitioner is so exceedingly important GOD UNLIMITED has scheduled the training of its candidates for this field to complete their training for both ministerial and practitioner studies at the same time leading to both recognitions. Whether a *Practitioner* carries out the church relationship of the minister is up to each one, but all practitioners are ministering to their people. In the same relationship, all ministers are practitioners in all their relationships.

The *Practitioner* is totally and **always only concerned with his own state of awareness** recognizing the world he lives in is pure and perfect. In this integrity and sincerity he can effectively "treat" and place a new cause in motion relative to his people for their highest good.

Since ministers and practitioners of the Church of God Unlimited work internationally, each is responsible to register as required by the local governmental agencies and to live within the regulations as promulgated by those offices with respect to the conduct of being a minister and practitioner in those cities, counties, states, governmental jurisdictions in whatever nation each professional is active.

It is recognized that when a professional knows the realm within which he operates, he can be a much more effective practitioner of his art.

*E*ach minister and practitioner is responsible to know the "laws" governing his activities within any given legal jurisdication and to abide by them.

The *Practitioner* has a further role in the community and in his world—that role is one of CREATOR.

The *Practitioner* creates the community in which he lives and the world which surrounds him. He does this as effectively as the infinite brought all things into being. The *Practitioner* does this by his awareness of who and what he is, who and what the world is, and who and what his fellow creatures are!

This is quite a sizable awareness. It does not brook of irresponsibility on the part of the *Practitioner*. It means business! It means that every thought that passes through an *effective* practitioner's mind brings about results that are as definite as the eternal beingness of all.

This seems like something that only a very knowledgeable and proven professional in a field might encounter. It seems like something that only the *top brass* are expected to know—but NO, all who are the practitioners of life not only must know these principles, but actually actuate them whether they do so knowingly or unknowingly.

None can escape the responsibility for their thought, their word and their action. This is a world in which the very ethers respond to our impulse from the mental, physical and spiritual aspects of our being so powerfully and wonderfully, that we had best be about our Father's business of taking total responsibility for our thought, word and action.

The *Practitioner* is one who has studied these eternal principles and takes the responsibility for his word and action and, of course, brings about a world so wondrously joyous, so marvelously attractive, so compellingly beautiful—others call him a master, a sage, a guru or any other term of endearment—but in truth he is just being that which we are all designed to be, effective utilizers of our total being, our God nature to its fullest, for WE ARE GOD!

The role of the *Practitioner* is a very definite one. If we choose to live within that framework, we can expect a mighty pleasing life. We can expect that our world will be filled with joy and abundance. We can expect that everyone we greet in this wondrous world which we have created will outpicture the perfection which we are and which they are and always have been.

It is a title we cannot assume lightly. It is a title which everyman has right now. Some live knowingly of this title, others live in ignorance of the truth of their being, but the truth is the title sticks—everyman is a practitioner right now. We, in assuming this role consciously, have the privilege of knowing it and enacting the privileges of this experience fully.

∞

To believe in
God
Is to yearn for
His existence.

Miguel de Unamuno

A MINISTER,
A LIVING EXAMPLE

A minister shares with his congregation *as a living example.* He chooses the task of minister to share *inner wisdom.* He creates a church *and a congregation* for the recognition of being one. The minister dwells in a pure state of consciousness untouched by worldly appearances. He lives Jesus' words: *Be ye therefore perfect, even as your Father which is in heaven is perfect.* [3]

A minister practices what he has studied. After hours of diligent study, following his inner calling

---

[3]   Matthew 5:48 [KJV]

to be a minister, he is ordained a minister to joyously open his church. His sharing is based on his inner knowingness, his reality: *I am God, God I am.*

With the decision to live this uplifting God-path, the selfdedicated student takes the first sip of spiritual water titillating his ethereal thirst. From the *Art & Science of Wholeness* the minister learned to renew his knowingness about the unchangeable truth and shares it with his congregation. He lives the unlimitedness of GOD.

Illumined by his new awareness he recognizes God's omniscience, omnipresence, omnipotence. He lives the terms: God unlimitedness, indivisible and unchangeable in all its expression.

The newly ordained minister knows God is all, he is God as well as everyone else. He sees God in all his congregation, in every individual joining his assembly. His sharing is neither teaching nor tutoring, but as a perfect living example. In all his sharing he refers to principle.

A minister shares with his congregation introspectively. He carries out his daily task based on his commitment to his own joy. As God is all, he lives in that consciousness of ubiquitousness radiating confidence to all the world. His belief is based on inner wisdom, unconditional love and mutual respect—while being a living example to the congregation. With selfconfidence he sees the church growing.

A wellknown philosopher and minister, as a young man, gave classes in a church for weeks but none came to listen. His mother heard about it and went to encourage him on his excellent lectures.

She did not give up on her son. She knew (she too was a minister) that her son did not need any credit for his magnificence. He talked for the joy of letting his inner wisdom shine forth and he did it happily for himself. Growth followed.

We are our own master, our own minister. Our church, our congregation, is our inner world. We know God in every expression on earth and we are unlimited, untouched by any outer appearance. A minister creates his world according to his inner knowingness and shares unlimited God wherever he is.

The congregation of a minister may be small or large, the minister creates it according to his consciousness. He shares by being himself and having fun—a most glorious, charismatic living example. He is one as his church, he is one as his congregation.

DEFINITION OF PRACTITIONER

*P*ractitioner is the qualification given to one who is engaged in a profession requiring special training as does for example the profession of lawyer, physician, consultant, teacher, parent need specialized knowledge and diligent application.

Work Of The Minister/Practitioner

A successful metaphysical practitioner is at peace within himself and looks in a positive way at whatever situation or experience he creates in his life. It is worthwhile and rewarding to think that all relative life is a wonderful funfilled game of following a calling.

A minister/practitioner thinks of himself whatever he thinks of another person.

A minister/practitioner does for himself whatever he thinks of doing for a friend.

Every minister is a practitioner in his own life of his beliefs.

As a public person the minister eagerly creates harmonious relationships in every corner of his world. Each minister/practitioner conducts his work in the first person, present tense, positive.

A minister counsels and treats. A practitioner only treats.

Creating Harmonious Relationships

*A*ll begins in consciousness resulting in the behavior each individual professes.

The minister/practitioner in the Church of God Unlimited knows who he is, professes the God concept and affirms to himself: I am God, God I am.

Harmony is a stage of pure consciousness the minister/practitioner creates in acknowledging formally the truth about himself. He believes in himself and supports his convictions with positive statements of wholeness, integrity and perfection.

He stands true to principle and performs his ministerial and healing work in an attitude of balance, harmony and overwhelming love for all.

Healing is the effect of affirming first to oneself the original purity, wholeness and integrity and then visualizing the effect in the friend. The essence of these divine qualities is inherent in mankind eagerly waiting for the sincere call to manifest.

The task of a minister is to take care of the clerical and administrative duties with diligence and harmony. The minister pays regular visits to the parishioners, his supporters. He fulfills the obligations in serving as listed in the regulations of his church. He conducts the worship service on Sundays as well as on official holidays. He teaches classes and counsels whoever calls upon him.

The minister is a welcome guest whenever he pays a visit to the parishioners. These visits are a blessing and inspiration for everybody.

The practitioner, calm and humble, is a valuable assistant to the minister in his work.

When the minister counsels with a friend, he wisely asks questions about what the friend wants and what is his true desire. He lovingly gives good illustrations of parallel or similar cases. In this way the friend finds the solution he considers appropriate for himself.

The minister sees the friend, who asks for healing, receptive to what he believes about himself. Then he puts a cause in motion for the specific desire the friend has. He treats with the friend in the conviction of the words of Jesus: *It is done unto you according to your belief.* 4

The minister respects the belief and free choice of the friend. It is up to the friend to find the solution which is acceptable to him.

Metaphysical Practitioner's Role

A practitioner of God Unlimited/University of Healing has successfully accomplished training in metaphysics for the role of being a philosophical-metaphysical practitioner for himself and the world about him. This means he is the CREATOR of his relative world, his spiritual life and the rewarding experiences he gains in both areas. His primary concern and achievement is: being true to himself and having fun in whatever he does.

Through the use of meditation, positive truth statements, awareness of being God, peace and love he partakes of the infinite abundance of the universe. With his thoughts and words the practitioner creates things and events he claims for himself.

A practitioner is a light and an inspiring example of his belief and goodness, and a blessing to all his creation in his community.

A practitioner lives from his inner creative center of inspiration. He listens to his inner voice

---

4   Matthew 9:29 [KJV]

and does not rationalize about the convenience or burden of carrying out what the friend asks.

As a practitioner is true to himself, he cannot be false to anyone. Hence the practitioner is a living example by being steadfast in his belief and lives accordingly to the eternal principles.

He works with the Law of cause and effect and knows that this universal Law works perfectly to manifest whatever he claims speaking his word or thinking his thought. The Law processes without evaluating or judging the things which are claimed. All is God, all is good, beneficial and meaningful. His way of living is a resplendent expression of God's omnipresence, omniscience and omnipotence.

The eyes of the practitioner are the open windows of his consciousness. It is a mirror of truth, the eternal truth of divine qualities which are firmly anchored in his consciousness. Whosoever looks attentively in that kind of mirror sees the reflection of his own qualities of unconditional love, goodness, harmony, abundance and wisdom.

Everybody Is A Practitioner

A practitioner proclaims: unconditional love and inner harmony are the foundation of a successful, harmonious life. He tunes into his divine self, follows his inner voice, the voice of truth and intuition and experiences a glorious fulfilling life.

Everyone has freedom of choice to believing in himself and practicing whatever he feels is the best solution in achieving a specific result.

A young boy was injured by a tractor and lost the use of his legs. The opinion of the doctors was that the boy could never walk again. His mother, however, believed that anything is possible. Through the hours of the night she affirmed: *I see you whole and perfect. I see you walking, running and playing on your perfect legs.* For several weeks she held her evening treatment vigil at the boy's bedside as he slept unaware of his mother's prac- titioner statement. All the while she massaged his legs with infinite love and motivated him to walk. The boy succeeded to use his legs perfectly. Choice! Using the Law of cause and effect. A great practitioner.   ∞

The sky
Is the
Daily bread
Of the
Eyes.

Ralph Waldo Emerson

Theme 3

CHURCHES

THE *FIRST*
TEN COMMANDMENTS

I   *I am One God, there is only One.*

II   *I create everything that is created.*

III   *Everything I create is Good.*

IV   *I create man to be me and I like me.*

V   *All that I am man is, in an eternally perfect body.*

VI   *I give man freedom of choice.*

VII   *I create man to be true to himself and have fun being himself.*

VIII   *Man lives within the Law of Cause and Effect.*

IX   *Since I am man, man is God and acts as God in everything he does.*

X   *I am omniscient, omnipotent and omnipresent and so is all of mankind.*

(Commandment: Power to take dominion)

The first TEN COMMANDMENTS God gave Moses on Mt Sinai.

The end of life
Is to be like God
And the soul
Following God
Will be like Him.

Socrates

SUCCESSFUL CHURCHES

*E*very student, member of the congregation and minister may live by the teachings of the *Master Teacher Within.* As Jesus the Christ said: *It is not I but the Father that dwelleth in me, he doeth the works.*[1]—so we teach everyone how to contact the Father within who doeth the works.

Church services and classes are for instruction, illumination and inspiration, showing that each is not alone on his pathway to truth. This is the real act of worship.

---

1   John 14:10 [KJV]

The church is a sharing, meditating, teaching, preaching and healing center.

If Sunday services are weak it is because the minister is ineffective in his speaking. People could go to any church or lecture but come to hear one minister because that minister inspires them to confident action. The effective minister possesses strong qualities of leadership, inspiration and showmanship. To old time religionists this would sound *unworthy* but a minister feels guided, led, *called,* to go forth to preach, teach and heal and if he is to be successful he must be able to retain a following. He experiences one hundred percent Sunday church attendance and class attendance of his membership as he meets the needs of his people. This need is to demonstrate more complete and fulfilling lives; in other words, to demonstrate and manifest good in every avenue of their lives.

Great ministers do that today in their churches. Every minister is a great speaker *as he believes in himself* as he believes in God in him as him.

The Sunday morning congregation is a fair measure of the people's interest in their church and its leader. Their interest in their church is a fair measure of their interest in God within each of them.

The minister has another barometer which tells the story of how well he is meeting the needs of his congregation—this is the ballot box. Every Sunday the congregation cast their ballot either in favor or against the minister's approach with their green stuff. Each piece of currency is a vote in favor of the minister's approach to religion, life and the divinity of all.

One of the ways to have a successful ministry is to use every asset one has available. Every church should have active practitioners. These practitioners should not only work with friends and their needs—but abundantly for the church; for the minister; and for the classes and other activities of the church. Their effective ministrations will reap a harvest of fabulous success for the minister and the church, the Sunday school, the classes, and the outreach of the church in the community. All are needed. The leader could do it alone but in areas where he is not as strong as he might be, help is in order.

The minister should use all the local media: radio, tv, newspapers, magazines, store bulletin boards, Chamber of Commerce, etc, telling of the services and classes and activities of the church. There is public service time available on all radio and tv stations, there is a signon and signoff time for tv which utilize local pastors giving the prayers, articles to newspapers and magazines plus of course—advertising. In sending out literature churches can use the Post Office Third Class Nonprofit mailing indicia. Also available is the Postal Library Rate for sending literature to members. Ask about details at your local post office.

The minister must be a friend of all and while doing business with them always see the *purity* in each one.

It is incumbent upon the minister to be involved in community activities to belong to service clubs, Chamber of Commerce, professional businessmen's organizations and the local ministerial association. Each of these bring him in contact with the community at large in which he is interested in serving.

Regular Sunday morning church services well planned and presented are unquestionably the very greatest blessing a community could have. It should be as significant, beautiful and inspirational as possible. It should use all the help it can get including sermon, singing, prayers, music and pageantry.

Prayers while important should not be too long. These tend to put the congregation out of the spirit of prayer. A number of short prayers interspersed in various parts of the service are most effective.

Many hymns are prayers, and most effective prayers too. Soft musical strains of prayer hymns are thought of as an expression of congregational communion. A good prayer well read is better than one where an illprepared minister appears to be wondering what to say.

A one hour service is sufficient. Twenty minutes for congregational singing, twenty minutes for the inspirational talk, twenty minutes for prayer, offering, announcements, etc.

If every aspect of the service is well prepared, all wasted time and useless talk and all valueless features are eliminated, only then is it a beautiful and helpful service, a precious hour in the lives of the people.

Congregational singing is one of the best features of a religious service. *A singing church is always well attended.* People love it. A singing church and a teaching pulpit. Church singing is a time for a "Hymn Sing" not at an hour of the day which proves undesirable for many and for which most people cannot attend. Congregational singing should not be shoved aside by an ambitious choir or a long winded leader.

A continuous song service is better than one interspersed by remarks of the leader. Sing the same songs often so people become familiar with them. It is the hymns we know that are the ones we love. And we never tire of the hymns we love. This type of church music is such a magnet to people you could not keep them away from the church door.

What a good choir can do for a church service is beyond description. But too often the pieces selected by the choir director are not music that responds to the metaphysical teachings of truth and voids the impact of the minister's talk. The words of the hymns must be correlated to the metaphysical teachings of the church. This is the responsibility of the minister to make sure this is done. Keep the old fashioned hymns, keep most of the words, but turn them to an uplifting direction rather than the former *hell fire and damnation type* of wording so frequent in many of the old hymns.

The metaphysical church must make the transition from the traditional Jesus-on-the-cross, to Jesus-the-master-teacher. It must be done. Recently women were emancipated from lives of much meaninglessness after they stood up and demanded their rightful place in life. So the minister must stand up so that the transition is found necessary and is done.

Preaching is an important ministry of the church. The spoken word is the main agency in extending the action of God among man but it should be teaching words. The pulpit is the teaching agency of the church held by ministers who live what they teach.

Twenty minutes for the talk, generally. True, a shorter talk requires greater preparation. No amount of gestures can atone for lack of ideas in a talk.

If a minister cannot learn to speak without continually halting hesitating and repeating, it would be better for him to write his talks and read them. A talk well written and well read may be delivered with as much force as if spoken off-hand. It is beautiful how much can be condensed into a small space when the subject is worked over and over, and written and rewritten and rewritten again. ∞

Judaism

Confucianism

Buddhism

Mohammedanism

Christianity

Hinduism

POSITIVE ATTITUDE
CREATES A
SUCCESSFUL CONGREGATION

A minister treats his congregation as he would like to be treated. He provides his parishioners with imaginative ideas which thrill him.

The *Ministers Manual* is a valuable reference book for the minister/practitioner.

A minister has a successful congregation because he shares the depth of his heart in what he does. He shares love with children, families, other churches and groups who look to his congregation as the ideal of spiritual service.

The congregation is a happy family as they are integrated in togethernesses by participating with enthusiasm, joy and expectation.

The church service shares that each one goes their unique pathway to truth. Teaching, healing and preaching inspire each individual to work within himself: *To let go and let God.*

The church is a spiritual center in which the congregation is inspired to act by understanding that God is within each one. By individually taking responsibility, God unlimited is experienced. The parishioner then believes in himself.

The minister shares with his congregation the idea of healing. The minister is not the healer, he helps the friend to recognize perfect wholeness and manifest it. The minister reminds his congregation that healing is defined: to return to our original purity and integrity.[2] Everyone can return because he has mentally left his original state of purity and integrity and can return to it by his choice. There is one universal Law, the Law of cause and effect. Every thought thought brings an effect. There are many spectacular healing successes in congregations since many recognize their spiritual wholeness and take over responsibility by choosing beneficial thought. The congregation affirms: I am all things. The minister teaches the Christ. Jesus said: *What will ye that I shall do unto you?;*[3] because his Christ consciousness saw only purity and perfection. This is what a minister/practitioner sees in everyone. A minister sees parishioners as practitioners because he sees wholeness and perfection in all.

---

2   Webster's Collegiate Dictionary
3   Matthew 20:32 or Mark 10:51 and Luke 18:41 [KJV]

A minister especially likes meetings during the week when many questions come up which are discussed in all openness. The minister's love of children shows as he enjoys their frank talks about their thought. What the minister and participants speak about in meetings inspires Sunday services and each offers ideas to work on during the week.

Music in a church service is uplifting. It raises the consciousness of all who take part in this spiritual meeting.

The word in each service is very important for inspiring thought. This thought is tried and true. It offers illumination.

The minister shares immortality thought with his congregation: Life is immortal. All is God. I am God. Jesus taught: *The last enemy that shall be destroyed is death.*[4]

A successful congregation is filled with parishioners who enjoy their wholeness and perfection and know that since all is God, everyone is God.

A minister is aware of his true nature when he says: I, as God, see all creation perfect. The minister's positive attitude creates a successful congregation that is convinced: God is all, I am all, all is all.

∞

---

4   I Corinthians 15:26 [KJV]

Those
Who have riches
Build temples
For Thee.

12th Century Hindu Psalm

WHY PEOPLE CHOOSE
A CERTAIN CHURCH

A survey in a suburban area of Houston Texas revealed what motivated people to choose a church:

3% — man in the pulpit

8% — architectural beauty of the building

12% — prior denominational affiliation

18% — convenience of location

20% — influenced by the fact that there were people in the congregation whom they respect.

BUT —

35% — *because their friends and neighbors invited them.*

Churches survive and grow because members have a story to tell and an invitation to extend.

This condition holds true with denominational churches and it could hold true with nondenominational and interdenominational churches as well. While the minister is the most effective drawing card a church can have providing the leadership, spiritual message, guidance and counseling of the people—it is the people who build a strong and lasting spiritual community within a church—for in the last analysis the church is the people and the people go on forever. Ministers come and go.   ∞

PROSPERITY

*A*bundance and prosperity are always in great demand. It seems that no matter how good things are going, we can always accept and receive more good and never have too much.

In working with GOD UNLIMITED we are truly working with the unlimited abundance of the universe, the unlimited supply of the infinite, of the unlimited sustenance of all.

When we work with our churches, recognizing that there is only one source and that source is God, we never beg from our parishioners or from those with whom we work. Rather we initiate the universal flow and our good is assured. We are not so much interested in abundance as we are in *unlimited financial stability* in our churches, our personal lives and in the lives of those with whom we are associated.

From this point of view we inform our people how they can give to our organization and further the work it is doing—but never with a sense of begging or of being in any kind of need. For always and only, *God is the source.*

We teach our people the act of tithing, not so much because it helps us, rather it builds a consciousness of wealth within them.

Bring ye all the tithes into the storehouse, that there may be meat in mine house, and prove me now herewith, saith the LORD *of hosts, if I will not open you the windows of heaven, and pour you out a blessing, that there shall not be room enough to receive it.*[5]

Thou shalt remember the Lord thy God: for it is he that giveth thee power to get wealth.[6]

As we teach our people tithing it is not in the usual manner. We teach them that as they give a tenth of *all* their income from whatever channel, to themselves first, to their happiness account and a tenth to the religious organization which helps them grow spiritually, they are fulfilling the Law. *For whosoever hath, to him shall be given, and he shall have more abundance: but whosoever has not, from him shall be taken away even that he hath.*[7] This Law of cause and effect is immutable

---

5   Malachi 3:10 [KJV]

6   Deuteronomy 8:18 [KJV]

7   Matthew 13:12 [KJV]

and that is the reason for the happiness account. When we have some good in our "account" we are never in want. If we do not have any good in our "account" then we feel bereft indeed of any abundance of good. Giving to the spiritual center that helps us reveal the divinity within is exceedingly important for this is our very "lifeline" with good, oftentimes, since we feel so separated in awareness from the universal principal of all good.   ∞

ABUNDANCE
BLESSING CARDS

*T*he following two cards are very effective we at the University of Healing and the Church of GOD UNLIMITED have found.

The one card lists the amount given by the individual, family or organization to the work of the church and the university. Recognizing in advance the divine source and rejoicing in advance for needs met.

The second card is appreciation from the spiritual center saying: *Your freewill love offering is greatly appreciated in support of our work.* From whence any good comes to the organization, thanks is given for that channel.

It is indeed representative of the one source through which the *source* extends its universal good to us. These can be changed to fit your own church and used by the givers and by the receivers.

International
Headquarters

God Unlimited
University of Healing

1101 Far Valley Road Campo CA 91906-3213

YES, ENCLOSED IS MY FREE WILL LOVE OFFERING OF

$_____

GLADLY GIVEN IN RECOGNITION OF THE DIVINE SOURCE, I AM JOINING
WITH YOU IN GIVING THANKS IN ADVANCE FOR ALL OF MY NEEDS MET.

Signed _____

International
Headquarters

God Unlimited
University of Healing

1101 Far Valley Road Campo CA 91906-3213

THANK YOU FOR YOUR OFFERING OF **$**_____

PEACE BE WITH YOU.

CHURCH TREASURER

DATE _____

∞

GIFTS BLESS THE GIVER

*G*ifts come in many guises as love from the infinite source.

The kinds of gifts given and received are many and the benefits of giving generously and receiving bountifully are truly gratifying and represent one of the noble traditions in the human spirit. These include bequests, legacies, devises, transfers of stock and other gifts.

The kind of gift your people utilize in supporting your church is both an expression of their generosity and their willingness to share something of value which they have with you.

All gifts that are given to the Church of God Unlimited, the University of Healing or to member churches as charitable gifts are tax deductible. The amount of deductible value varies with the kind and timing of their gift. **These rules change often, check first with your tax advisor.**

As a rule of thumb your parishioners can figure if their tax rate is thirty percent, their taxes will be reduced by thirty percent of the amount of their gift. So it may be noted that if a gift of $1,000 is given this would reduce their taxes by thirty percent and actually cost the giver only $700 in actual cash. This is based on a married person filing jointly. For a single person and head of households the real deduction may even be exceedingly larger.

A gift of stocks, bonds, etc—securities—generates a deduction which is equal to the full market value of these securities. Also, appreciated securities held longer than six months bypass capital gains taxes when given. So if your parishioner has a stock which he bought five years ago for $200 and it is now valued at $1,000, selling it he would be liable for capital gains tax on the $800 profit. Instead, giving them to the church as a gift he may deduct the entire $1,000 as a gift and pay no capital gains tax at all.

A gift of real estate including residential, commercial, unimproved land and income property can be one of the most imaginative ways of making a gift. Appreciated property held longer than six months and given to the church allows the donor to receive an immediate charitable deduction and thereby avoid all capital gains taxes on the gift.

When your parishioners have gifts of tangible personal property such as books, paintings, antiques or other items, these are subject to similar advantageous tax rules as gifts of appreciated property and securities. A collection of rare books to the church library allows the donor to claim as a charitable contribution the fair market value of the books as established by an independent appraiser.

For those parishioners who want to honor a deceased loved one or friend, a memorial gift to the church is a thoughtful way to do so. Families of those whose memories they have honored will be notified by an appropriate card, as will the church's acknowledgment of the gift.

A charitable trust can be created by an irrevocable transfer of money or property to a trust for the benefit of their church, in exchange for a return of income. One or more individuals may receive trust earnings as beneficiaries. At the death of the last surviving beneficiary, the trust terminates and the assets are transferred to the church. Substantial tax advantages can be permitted the donor, including a charitable deduction, complete avoidance of capital gains taxes, reduction of estate taxes, and possible favorable tax treatment on the earnings of the trust.

A gift in the parishioner's will is a considerable expression of a lifelong effort. The gift may have tax consequences and does not affect the donor's current income.

A gift of a life insurance policy can be an attractive way to make a substantial gift. A charitable deduction is allowed which is approximate to the cash value of the policy. In addition deductions are allowed if you continue to pay the premiums after making the gift. The testamentary trust provides a significant gift which may be realized when the donor establishes a trust under his will naming the church as the remainder man. Income from the trust can be designated to one or more individuals for a term of years.

Letting your people know about these techniques of giving which benefit them in many ways is vitally important and one of the responsible duties of a church administrator—minister—practitioner.

Always remember, though, God is the one and only source.

Remembering this, you will not be tempted to cowtow to an individual or circumstance for your good.

God is the source!

CONTRIBUTION LETTER TO GIVERS

International Headquarters

2001 BLESSINGS

Mr and Mrs Independently Wealthy
711 Abundance Way
Source, God 91906—3213

Dear Mr and Mrs Wealthy

During the year 2001 you have blessed God Unlimited/University of Healing with your love offerings in sponsorship of our many activities.

We love and bless you for the gifts you have given to maintain our ministry.

GOD UNLIMITED is a church of meditation, teaching and healing, revealing man's divine splendor within. A county, state and federally tax exempt nonprofit religious, educational and charitable corporation working as an international and interdenominational church serving around the world through the University of Healing with the work of the church, campus meditation center, ORDER OF ABSOLUTE, Absolute Monastery and the University entirely financed by voluntary contributions which are income tax deductible.

Bequests, legacies, devises, transfers of stock and other gifts for the use of God Unlimited/University of Healing are deductible from State, Federal, Estate and Gift Tax purposes.

GOD UNLIMITED teaches the divinity of man, scientifically proven prayer treatment effective in every avenue of one's life and the oneness of all life.

GOD UNLIMITED reveals the eternal principles through which every person may know their inherent divinity and purity, may live a more fulfilled life and better understand their fellow being.

Your freely given love offering for 2001 in the amount of $ _____ is greatly appreciated.

Thank you.

Love and blessings

Peace

Dr Ellen Jermini
Treasurer

How excellent
Are thy designs
O lord
Of eternity

12th Century Hindu Psalm

STARTING A CHURCH
IN A NEW COMMUNITY

*O*ne of the greatest experiences in the life of any minister is founding a church in a community where there had been no church of his persuasion before. To effectively establish a church in any community requires research on the part of the minister.

If you have made the decision to move to a community because your family has employment there, your children want to be in school there, your relatives or friends live there, or whatever—*then* the reason you have chosen to move to that community is specifically to establish a church there even though you did not know it.

Decide for yourself at the outset, how large would you like to have *your* church. Then the next question is whether that community could support a nontraditional interdenominational church with either a large number of new thought thinkers, independent minds, a special community like a university center or something of that nature which does not focus itself around the traditional affects of religion and philosophy, but activates itself into creative avenues of experience.

WHO Do We Attract

*O*nce you determine the community in which you desire to found a church your next step is to determine the neighborhood in which you would like to build up the image of your philosophical religious affectation. The adage, *we are known by the company we keep,* is never more true than with a church.

Locating near the educational centers, near the industrial or financial centers, or in suburban areas—all are indicative of the type of people who will feel sympathetic to your endeavor. You are not seeking "class" structure, or "holier (better) than thou" people—but what you are seeking to do is to reach those people who have personal integrity and courage to claim their oneness as God, their heirship as the infinite and their outpicturing of their God nature—I AM GOD! This takes intestinal fortitude as well as social and business courage.

So placing your spiritual center of learning, your church home, in a location where it will both invite the level of consciousness empathetic with truth as well as to attract those people who want to experience the greater fulfillment which life has in store for them of abundance, happiness, health, success, right action, more harmonious affairs and business integrity, is of utmost importance.

Once you select the neighborhood check with the city building authorities to see what buildings might serve as your "first home" in that city in that area. Those building inspectors and officials are very helpful because they want to avoid misunderstandings and often can give you leads you might not have dreamed of without their counsel.

Check Area Merchants

*A*fter checking there and following their leads, be sure to go to the local merchants and tell them what you have in mind and where you have considered locating. They may have even better suggestions and your contacting them will open the doorway for drawing them into your group plus promoting your church in their stores and businesses. Check with each of the local real estate offices, not only one, for each office has listings of available properties not even known to the other offices. You do not owe allegiance to any broker but you owe it to yourself to do a thorough job of investigating sources for your church home. It will be the first of several as you expand and grow!

It pays to investigate possibly using the city school, community rooms or city recreation center as well as the meeting rooms in the bank or major department stores which are often available at no charge.

Make sure you meet the local Chamber of Commerce and the heads of the most prominent service clubs. Meet the ministers of the other churches and let them know that you are "coming aboard." You will be surprised how often they will be more than helpful to you in becoming established. Often, too, they might offer to share their facilities with YOU until you become established— and sometimes even on a long term basis. All very desirable.

Check out the use of the library, the local elementary and high school, as well as private schools, for the use of their facilities. These are often very reasonable and very desirable. Your use of their facilities is on a day they are usually not using them.

Check with the businessmen and residents of the area in which you desire to locate and see which newspaper they actually subscribe to and read it everyday. Do not use the information from the local newspaper. It may not be realistic. Check locally. Then investigate which newspaper is circulated effectively to the *areas of the community in which people live whom you might like to attract* to your church. After a careful investigation, determine in which papers you want to advertise and which days are best for your ad to appear. Then use it when the time is right.

Who Do You Attract

*L*iving by this statement momentarily you will find that it will manifest itself in your life and affairs. Let no setbacks deter you from the truth about yourself. You are successful, prosperous and inspirational—you build a successful congregation of regular attending and supportive members. Know this as your right in carrying on the work **God in you ordained for you to do.**

In the location you choose for a "church center" have something which makes it special for your group. If you have a banner with the name of your church on it available from church supply houses, all to the good. If you have a symbol that means something to your group, good. One group has the name of *Jonathan Chapel* and has a beautiful seagull on a stand as a symbol of their unlimitedness, other groups use the cross, the fish, the traditional symbols of Christianity, use whatever talks to your group. Use this at your podium or altar. Keep away from aping the traditional church.

Seek to have music with all your services either piano, organ or recorded music on disk. You can have your favorite hymns on CD (Compact Disk)—with or without words. This way you have the best of all worlds. This can be very effective. Some churches who end up on Sunday morning without a musician find it valuable to have it ready in case of a need. Have helpers to operate the various supports of the service so you are not doing everything.

Develop a statement of truth for yourself and use it continuously, such as:

I release myself to fulfilling God's desire in me as me through me. God in me inspired me to have a church in (name of community) and I release its total success and direction to God indwelling. I now know the right location. I am a successful minister serving this congregation. Our congregation supports our church in many ways. God is the course of our abundance and growth. I accept this is true and so it is.

I dedicate my
Consciousness
To remaining
True to the divine;
In my church
Every soul is sacred
And every man
Is divine!

How often
We look upon God
As our last and
Feeblest resource!
We go to him
Because we have
Nowhere else to go.
And then we learn
That the storms of life
Have driven us,
Not upon the rocks,
But into
The desired haven.

George McDonald

Theme 4

HEALING

TEACHING TREATMENT

*T*eaching treatment is teaching the responsibility and potentiality of the individual to heal himself. It is sharing the awareness that in our consciousness we are our own energy generator and that in balancing our vibrations we are healed.

One who has achieved this inner balance can generate such harmonious vibrations that each one who comes into his presence is uplifted—but it lasts only as long as the charisma of his presence continues.

"I experienced this during seminars of the University of Healing in Switzerland," said a seminar participant. "I was full of anxiety and depression at that time, but when I left the seminars I was floating on clouds of lightness, vibrating with new energy. The high lasted for a few days, but then slowly, like a drug that is withdrawn I fell into my old feelings and I was longing for the next seminar to fill myself with this marvelous energy again. Happily Dean Beierle taught us how to find this source of unlimited energy within ourselves and today I can keep up this energy level myself."

The purpose of teaching treatment is to share this technique to heal ourselves.

Important in teaching treatment is to share the awareness that we are divinely created and that within each one of us is the archetypally perfect pattern. Healing is returning to this perfection, the recognition and acceptance of it within ourselves. This can be done in an instant—we call it spontaneous healing—or it can evolve slowly in a steady growing in awareness, whatever we choose.

It is helpful to give illustrations where treatment in like cases has worked. A powerful way of having helpful examples ready is to write them down in categories like: Relationships, Peace, Healing, Abundance etc.

The practitioner is always a living example of being onepointed on the issue of wholeness, always knowing affirmations of truth function perfectly and maintaining an attitude of success regarding each treatment. The statement: *We teach best what we most need to learn*, bears itself out here. For, being a practitioner, we speak our word and healing is complete. However, when we must "teach" others we limit our effectiveness as a practitioner.

Thoughts Leading To
The Awareness Of Our
Original Perfection

*I*n teaching treatment it is most important to point out the importance of speaking treatment affirmations in first person, present tense, positive.

I affirm the truth: God is energy, I am energy, I direct energy by my attitude, my thought.

I affirm the truth: I live in a positive harmonious thought; vibrating with love, respect, joy and laughter; my divine reality generates well-functioning glands and organs in my body.

I affirm the truth: My body is the temple of the living God, my body is my home and my home is wherever I am. Every organ action and function of my body is perfect. I am the pure white light of love and my body is love.

I affirm the truth: I meditate on the thought of my perfection.

Treatment works through principle. We treat with our attention on perfection, we point out the solution we want to experience and who and what we are: God as wholeness and perfection revealed through us.

In teaching treatment, while it is important to share the concept of living affirmations in the first person, present thense, positive—it is even more important to be an example of how one lives in the first person, present tense, positive everyday world. Herein the miracles take place.

A Prayer of Wholeness

My world outpictures that which I live: the purity of my consciousness. My world is peace, beauty, harmony, wholeness, abundance. This is what I am. This is my reality.

My body is the demonstration of my reality. From any vantage point, I am all. I am the unlimited expression of the allness that I am. I am perfect, pure, vital, alive and immortal.

I enjoy everything as my conscious creation of love.

My body is the precious instrument of the one-pointed, disciplined expression of my divinity. I am whole spiritually, mentally and physically. With every thought I think I demonstrate the reality of my existence. My body intrinsically reflects the concept, idea and thought I hold in my consciousness. I am thought expressing as wholeness, perfection, health, abundance, harmony, love and perfect peace. These facts are affirmations of my archetypal being, the spiritual food I give my mind about my body.

∞

HEALING SERVICE

*S*ome ministers/practitioners have concern over the thought, *What if I held a healing service and nothing happened?*

He who makes the experiment will have the experience.

The minister/practitioner is the instrument God uses to manifest that which is the birthight of every individual—the action of Law. When the minister begins a healing service all that is needed are the people. Then healings take place. The minister is the catalyst who activates the minds of the people inward, godward, and sets in motion the Law of cause and effect to accomplish the great good desired.

Often it is not the first session in which healings take place. But as the conviction grows on the part of the people and the minister, great things happen. The faith and confidence of the people are rewarded. How much more effective is a healing service when both people and minister/practitioner come to the service with absolute faith and expectation.

Illness is the result of our nonbeneficial use of the Law of cause and effect. Health is our gift from the beneficial use of the Law of cause and effect. When we suffer illness all that need be done is to place a new cause in motion to bring about the desired result. This means that a person receives experiences in his life because he has mentally placed the condition in motion to bring it about. So if there is a hurricane, flood, disaster, illness, poverty, unhappiness, or whatever it may be, by knowing you are the perfection of God and enfolded in its love, a thousand shall fall at thy side, and ten thousand at thy right hand; but it shall not come nigh thee.[1] But should your consciousness slip for a moment and you have the experience—at the moment you become conscious of your "slipping" you can change the cause and execute an entirely new condition—wholeness once again!

All are channels for the healing experience. Every clergyman, by the fact that he has dedicated

---

1   Psalms 91:7 [KJV]

his life to knowing the truth, is a healing channel and a very active one!

While the minister/practitioner work cooperatively with the medical practitioner, medical proofs are difficult to amass on spiritual healings. Medical records are usually unavailable from hospital files involved and most of the time they state simply "it may have been a wrong diagnosis" or that it is always possible for a specific disease to evidence "spontaneous remission." But these proofs are really not needed since the practitioner works with principle and when the friend is healed this is proof enough that the Law has done its work. The gift of God$_2$, given before the beginning, of a perfect man is verified by the healing which takes place, whomsoever is given the "credit" or reward.

The minister makes sure the friend has seen a doctor and is seeing one unless discharged as terminal or "hopeless." The minister and the doctor are two examples of the approaches to wholeness.   ∞

---

2   "And God said, Let us make man in our image, after our likeness; and let them have dominion . . . over all the earth . . . And God saw everything that he had made, and, behold, it was very good." Genesis 1:26,31. [KJV]

There is a power for good
In the universe . . .
Available to everyone.
And you can use it

Ernest Holmes

GOD UNLIMITED HEALING

*I*t is desirable in every church to establish a prayer group, a silent healing ministry, a group which meets at specific times at the church or in their homes, together or absently, at a specific time to treat and to pray for the manifestation of perfection in those who have asked for this treatment. With this foundation of confident healing oriented people in your church having healing services will prove most beneficial and effective with these confident believers backing up the catalytic effort you make.

We have the Worldwide Healing Ministry of the Church of God Unlimited for this purpose at the Absolute Monastery.

As psychology is a systematic study of animal and human behavior, so in spiritual healing we apply spiritual principles such as the Law of cause and effect, love, prayer, awareness, faith, knowingness, to the healing of the body, mind and spirit. In its fullness, spiritual healing involves a personal relationship with God and draws the one who is healed into a fresh awareness of oneness as God.

From the work done by Jesus we see great emphasis was placed upon healing. Properly understood healing includes spirit, mind and body— the basic ministry of the church is healing. Jesus gave attention to bodily healing in his ministry, much more than the church does today. Ministers have been commissioned by Jesus to "heal the sick"[3] and such is the primary ministry of the Church of God Unlimited.

As ministers we realize that God is the only source of healing or perfection within its creation. God uses many channels but still is the one source. As we thank God for healing from every channel, from doctors, nurses and practitioners as well as from the inner working of the spiritual reality within man, we have opened ourselves to the allness of God at work. Nothing happens save through the direction of the eternal Law which is also God and coeternal with it. As we recognize this, our work as practitioners of the art of healing is to put the Law into practice.

---

3   Luke 9:2 [KJV]

As practitioners of healing we sometimes feel that our high hopes and unfulfilled expectations will react in a loss of faith and therefore in a loss to the church. This could be experienced, but not necessarily. We cannot guarantee healings for everyone, not even for someone, for as Jesus said, *According to YOUR faith be it unto you.*[4] *Not* the healer's faith but the friend's.

All spiritually mature people have prayed and found that sincere prayer is answered!

When people pray they have or are coming to learn that when they use the Law in an unbeneficial way, they benefit in a way that is unsatisfactory to them. Practicing spiritual healing helps strengthen and develop faith and knowingness which results in healing.

*W*e are not the healers; God has already given perfection from the beginning, we encourage the friend to recognize it within and draw it into manifest presence by healing our thought. We draw it into manifest presence by healing **our thought.**

At a public healing service the main emphasis is on instruction, not miracles, for a healing service is a specialized prayer meeting which takes

---

4   Matthew 9:29 [KJV]

the promise of *the Christ* at face value, *Ask, and it shall be given you; seek, and ye shall find; knock, and it shall be opened unto you; For every one that asketh receiveth; and he that seeketh findeth, and to him that knocketh it shall be opened.*[5]

Go thy way; and as thou hast believed, so be it done unto thee.[6]

Then it is truly done unto the friend according to his belief: The friend's ability to receive healing has nothing to do with God's givingness. ∞

---

5   Matthew 7:7-8 [KJV]

6   Matthew 8:13 [KJV]

As a countenance
Is made beautiful
By the soul's
Shining through it
So the world is beautified
By the shining
Through it of God.

Frederich Jacobi

HEALING POWER WITHIN

A minister/practitioner has the charisma of healing in his hands. The power that passes through each one is very definitely affected by his behavior and habit.

While very little is known about the specific properties of this power, it is part of the divine spirit of all men. To be used, and used continuously as a manifest channel of it, the practitioner has to live as "close to God" in awareness as he possibly can.

Be ye therefore perfect, even as your father which is in heaven is perfect.[7]

---

7   Mathew 5:48 [KJV]

We are all at different stages of development and understanding, and we are only expected to be true to ourselves and the knowledge given to us.

The results of healing often vary because of the channel's lack of confidence, but mostly because the friend continually returns to the negative cause.

Let Go And Let God

*A*s one is truly being used as a channel of this God power the channel becomes more free flowing as it is used.

If a practitioner is exhausted by what he does, then he is certainly not using the true power. The divine power never depletes anyone while it is being used. The power often varies and is closely related to the practice of selfdiscipline. It is affected by smoking. Smoking does not calm the senses, on the other hand, prayer does. Correct diet is of tremendous importance in working with healing. As natural a food as wine may be it clouds the mind and in practitioner work you need the clearest mind possible. Just as one would not want a medical doctor to have a drink before an operation, so a practitioner should be clear and alert to his God nature unobstructed by any outer stimulus. Fasting has been known to be beneficial for a practitioner in the art of healing.

All of these outward symbols are far less important than the state of mind of the practitioner. While his awareness is bound to be affected by anxiety or tension, if he is angry, has an upset at home, business problems, all these actively block his usefulness as spirit. This is why the Christ maintained a pure attitude of mind and body to achieve such amazing results.

Oneness With The Eternal

A healing ministry in a church does many things for the church, the parishioners, the minister/practitioner and for those who come in need and may not yet be associated with the church. There is a community of believers in a healing group directing all of their energies to one purpose—oneness with the eternal. Those who join the group for prayer and treatment feel this awareness and join in the sincerity of the group and are benefited from it. Then too, the members of the healing group begin helping one another with their needs and the minister's work is spread over the larger group and an effective healing ministry is brought forth.

The minister/practitioner is not the healer—the healer is the individual claiming the TRUTH about himself. In this way the healing ministry, individual and minister, are channels and catalysts of the healing art affected within each participant.

We live eternally. Our expectation is to be whole in spirit, mind and body. Healing is not synonymous with changing the effect which is recognized. The true cause behind many of the problems we face in life could be entirely different from what we expect. Attitudes of spiritual immaturity, being rebellious toward God and indifferent toward our spiritual reality—these may well be the real cause which has brought about the illness, poverty or lack of happiness in our lives. Many healing services stimulate this awareness and change in our being and this is one of the greatest healings, even though the outer may not have been changed, yet, with this great inner change the outer follows—AND PERMANENTLY—when the acceptance of spiritual health is met the change takes place in the outer. The truth of spiritual health is the recognition that our body was perfect from the very beginning and can be outwardly again as soon as we visualize this perfection.

I Accept!

*T*he prerequisite for healing is an open and receptive mind aware of its heritage from God. Make the statement—I ACCEPT! Mean it and claim it and experience it. All who came to Jesus and said I ACCEPT were healed by their own faith and conviction.

So many people went to Jesus and asked for healing. Jesus looked at all and saw their purity and perfection, which is natural for his eyes could only perceive purity. After Jesus had asked them, *What will ye that I shall do unto you?*[8] and the petitioners said to Jesus, "I would be made whole"

---

8   Matthew 20:32 [KJV], Mark 10:51 KJV], Luke 18:41 [KJV]

then did he help them. Until any friend wants whole-ness enough to know what they are asking for—until that moment—they cannot have wholeness. For most of the time they merely want the pain to stop, the problem to disappear, the condition to change. *The light of the body is the eye: if therefore thine eye be single, thy whole body shall be full of light.*9 Once they have recognized they are perfect and see with these eyes of perfection, the undesired condition will no longer be SEEN by them and they will be experiencing only wholeness and perfection. Health and illness are both perfection.

All use the Law of cause and effect.

Use of the Law can be done for sickness or health. When a practitioner uses the Law for heal-ing **to benefit himself**, this does **NOT** destroy the use of the Law through his hands.

*Physician, heal thyself!*10

If a practitioner feels called upon to use his charismatic power in the laying on of hands for healing he will find God working through him in this feeling of warmness or coolness or tingling as "God's Power" heals. This "power" flowing through the practitioner is not the "healing power" of the eternal, but rather it is the acceptance of the friend of the spiritual charisma of the practitioner and of their own relationship to it. The practitioner does not HEAL nor does GOD heal, the INDIVIDUAL RETURNS HIS AWARENESS, TO HIS ORIGINAL PURITY AND INTEGRITY and is thereby made outwardly

---

9   Matthew 6:22 [KJV]

10   Luke 4:23 [KJV]

whole. **God gives no new gifts—all was given perfectly in the beginning.**

Healing is not a selfish act or desire, for Jesus told us to: *Be ye therefore perfect, even as your Father which is in heaven is perfect.*[11]

Jesus never taught that it was God's will for anything to be less than perfect, for anyone to suffer illness or lack, for anyone to suffer misfortune. The only record we have of the disciples lack of ability to heal was what Jesus called their *unbelief.*[12]

Relapses from health occur when the cause of the illness has not been eliminated. If the person is healed in any area of his life and then continues to do those things which brought about the "illness" in the first place, the "illness" will return—or something different but equally undesirable will manifest in the person's experience.

Spiritual Healing Complete

*T*he difference between spiritual healing and other types of "healing" is that spiritual healing is complete and affects every area of the person's life: mental, physical, emotional and spiritual. With spiritual healing the person no longer wants anything which is not for his highest good. He loses all

---

11   Matthew 5:48 [KJV]

12   Mark 6:6 [KJV]

desire for those things which would limit him and destroy his total well being.

On the other hand, "healing" which allows for a relapse is one which is a healing of the effect only and therefore not spiritually and eternally founded. While we make the statement that all things are spiritual, so then we must even say that those things which are undesirable in our lives are spiritual too because we brought them to us by the use of the Law. This is not recognizing that there is that which is eternal and that which is temporal. That which is eternal is real, and is our use of the word, spiritual. While that which is temporal is only an illusion and in our use of the word spiritual, spiritual only insofar as it outpictures that which is contained within the individual and his world picture for himself.

Healing ministries can only be carried on by the spiritually alive of any generation.

Medicine sustains—maintains—the house in which man lives.

Spiritual healing heals—returns to its original purity and integrity—the whole man, spirit, mind and body—the wholistic person.

There is no limit to spiritual healing.

All Is Healed

*T*here is evidence of healing the so-called incurable diseases of spirit, mind and body. But there is no such thing as an incurable disease. There are only incurable persons. Those who do not wish to be healed.

Spiritual healing does not distinguish between organic and functional diseases or between curable and incurable diseases.

It is the duty of the clergy to heal those with psychiatric ailments. He deals with guilt, with feelings of insecurity, with emotional disturbances. A sick soul can make a sick mind as easily as a sick mind can make a sick body.

The objective in spiritual healing is not necessarily, or even primarily, the healing of the body. It is the health of the whole being, the entire personality. Man's being is immortal.

Healing may mean a victory in a renewed life of the body, or it may mean a triumphant entry into the larger life of the spirit.

We can at all times affirm: *I live in my eternally perfect body.*   ∞

COLLECTIVE COMMUNION

*T*his collective communion is said in stanzas, as: **I am one with God, I am one with God, I am one with God today**. And so on through each line of the communion.

It can be used as a chant or with selected music. It is exceedingly effective and raises the consciousness of those who take part in this spiritually evolutionary act.

I am one with God

I am one with Peace

I am one with Love

I am one with Health

I am one with Strength

I am one with Joy

I am one with Myself

I am one with You

I am that which Thou Art

Thou art that which I am

I am that I am

I am God, God I am!

OUTLINE FOR HEALING AND MEDITATION MEETINGS

Note: *Have basket, paper and pencils ready at the door for treatment requests before opening the meeting. Use Treatment Request Cards.*

Healing and Meditation Meeting Activities

I   Premeeting Activities

- One-half hour of preparation

- Peaceful music all or part of the time

- Premeeting audible treatment or meditation period, if desired, from five to fifteen minutes, by leader, for group discussion

II   Meeting—approximately one hour

- Announcements

- Meditation

- Lesson or instruction period
  30-45 minutes

- Healing Treatment work period

- Ideas to dwell upon throughout the week
  so you can work together in sustained
  consciousness, a combined treatment
  work

III *Collection: Love Offering*

Note: *Offering may be taken between lessons and treatment or by leaving basket at the door for contributions. Always take an offering!*

TREATMENT REQUESTS
AND TREATMENT REPORTS

*A*s a treatment is requested of the minis-
ter/practitioner, the wholeness/health/
abundance/success **need** must be adequately
known. First ask the friend what is the POSITIVE
HEALING REQUESTED. Do not get involved in a reci-
tation of the ills or problems, rather confine the
study to **what healing is desired**. Then work can
be done.

The reason the request should only relate the
healing desired is that the Law of cause and effect
responds to what we say is the POSITIVE HEALING
REQUESTED and gives that for which we asked.

TREATMENT REQUEST

For: **Name** _____

Address _____ **City** _____

Phone _____ **Date** _____

Positive Healing Requested _____

_____

_____

_____

_____

From: **Name** _____ **Phone** _____

Address _____

God Unlimited/University of Healing, Worldwide Healing Ministry
1101 Far Valley Road, Campo CA 91906-3213 (619) 478-5111

After the healing has been experienced get a Treatment Report.

TREATMENT REPORT

For: **Name** _____

Address _____ **City** _____

Phone _____ **Date** _____

Healing Action Reported _____

_____

_____

_____

_____

From: **Name** _____ **Phone** _____

Address _____

God Unlimited/University of Healing, Worldwide Healing Ministry
1101 Far Valley Road, Campo CA 91906-3213 (619) 478-5111

God is the poet
Of the world
With tender patience
Leading it by His vision
Of Truth
Beauty and
Goodness.

Alfred North Whitehead

Theme 5

VOWS

ORDINATION

*O*rdinations received from other church movements, though legally valid, are not recognized as full ministerial status in the Church of God Unlimited. Those who hold such recognition must complete the undergraduate course of the University of Healing and its Ministerial Course before being recognized as a minister of the Church of God Unlimited or else they do not know the religious philosophy they newly represent.

Ordination is the highest ecclesiastical recognition given to a minister. It is a permanent ministerial status in any church and in the Church of God Unlimited which cannot be taken from the person to whom it has been granted, except through due process of Canon Law. Ordination is for those who have decided to dedicate their lives to the sharing of the GOD UNLIMITED beliefs and practices through teaching, preaching, healing and example. An ordained minister of the Church of God Unlimited has full ministerial authority in the church which calls him to be its minister. It is his responsibility to fulfill the office of minister of that church, so the church will always be a healthy, wholesome member in the family of GOD UNLIMITED churches.

Code Of Ethics

The following passages from the Bible constitute the basic principle upon which the ministry is founded. For the minister they offer the first concrete definitions of conduct and the fundamental rock on which he may anchor his thought.

- *Love the Lord thy God with all thy heart, and with all thy soul, and with all thy mind . . . . Love thy neighbor as thyself.*[1]

- *The Spirit of the Lord is upon me; because the Lord hath anointed me to preach good tidings unto the meek; he has sent me to bind up the brokenhearted, to proclaim liberty to the captives, and the opening of the prison to them that are bound; to proclaim the acceptable year of the Lord, and the*

---

1   Matthew 22:37, 39 [KJV]

day of our God, to comfort all that mourn.[2]

- *I have been made a minister, according to the gift of the grace of God given on to me by the effectual working of his power.*[3]

- *Feed the flock of God which is among you, taking the oversight thereof, not by constraint, but willingly; not for filthy lucre, but of a ready mind. Neither as being lords over God's heritage, but being ensamples to the flock.*[4]

- *As every man hath received the gift, even so minister the same one to another, as good stewards of the manifold grace of God.*[5]

- *Finally, brethren, whatsoever things are true, whatsoever things are honest, whatsoever things are just, whatsoever things are pure, whatsoever things are lovely, whatsoever things are of good report; if there be any praise, think on these things.*[6]

- *The greater thou art, the more humble thyself.*[7]

- *Other sheep have I, which are not of this fold.*[8]

---

2   Isaiah 61:1,2 [KJV]
3   Ephesians 3:7 [KJV]
4   I Peter 5:2,3 [KJV]
5   I Peter 4:10 [KJV]
6   I Philippians 4:8 [KJV]
7   Solomon 3:18 [KJV]
8   John 10:16 [KJV]

- *Have we not all one father? hath not one God created me?*[9]

- *Let your light so shine before men, that they may see your good works, and glorify your Father which is in heaven.*[10]

- *Neither do I condemn thee: go, and sin no more.*[11]

- *Let the counsel of thine own heart stand.*[12]

*T*he University of Healing Board of Regents and Church of God Unlimited Commission on Education grants a diploma showing one has satisfactorily completed the prescribed course of study required for ministers. The Board of Directors of God Unlimited/University of Healing accepts you as a minister and candidate for its church commission.

---

9   Malachi 2:10 [KJV]
10   Matthew 5:16 [KJV]
11   John 8:11[KJV]
12   Ecclesiasticens 37, 13 [KJV]

*R*ite of Ordination and *Vow of Selfdedication* stand as the keys to ethical standards by which the minister lives and functions in his office. These vows specifically are given here so that the minister may, through daily reading and continuous selfanalysis, determine whether or not he is in complete accord with the code he has vowed to exemplify.

RITE OF ORDINATION AND VOW OF SELFDEDICATION

*T*he following statements define the philosophy of the Church of God Unlimited, the University of Healing and ORDER OF ABSOLUTE/The Absolute Monastery for ordination and selfdedication:

- *There is one creative cause; one living spirit; absolute, self existent beingness which knows itself and I call this God.*

- *God is omnipresent, omniscient, omnipotent; indivisible; God is in, through and as all of its creation.*

- *All is God!*

- *God is absolutely good, pure and perfect.*

- *Since all is God, I am God and I am absolutely good, pure and perfect.*

- *Death, growing old, illness, lack or anything negative are not necessary; as I recognize the truth of my creative cause, these things are no longer in my life.*

- *I experience perfect physical, mental and spiritual health as I claim this everlasting truth about myself.*

- *God is without beginning or end. I am God and I am without beginning or end. My self is eternal, immortal and continues from planes of existence to planes of existence forever and ever expanding until my self finally reveals its native purity and perfection and oneness as God.*

- *Every individual self has the privilege being aware of its true nature. I, as God, see all creation as God sees it when I am unconditional loving, nonpossessive and nonjudgmental.*

- *I am a necessary expression of God.*

- *I love God, I love my fellowman as I love myself, therein, I express the supreme purpose for my existence.*

- *I know God by turning to the very center of my being, going within this quietness and peace and God in me as me reveals itself through me now.*

- *I know who I am and as an expression of God in its allness I say of myself: I AM GOD, GOD I AM!*

IT IS DONE

*T*HE CHURCH OF GOD UNLIMITED ministers are unique in that in addition to being a minister, a teacher, a counselor, they are also a practitioner. An ordained minister has acquired through training, a glimpse of what a minister should be. Experience brings the required wisdom, experience teaches the truisms that mellow and mature the minister as a human being and as a spiritual leader. The foregoing vows should be studied and observed as a guide to spiritual maturity.

The minister has chosen a profession wherein he becomes a balancing factor in the lives of his constituents. In order to do this effectively he must reflect in his own life precisely what he desires to elicit from those whom he serves.

In GOD UNLIMITED the minister is a therapist who specializes in the use of spiritual treatment. He uses the word practitioner, one who practices spiritual healing, with enthusiasm and joy.

We define the term vow and ministerial:

Vow—binding oneself to an act, service or condition; and

Ministerial—obedience to recognizing the purity within all men!

Anyone who achieves the *title* of Minister of the CHURCH OF GOD UNLIMITED is a balanced person. This balanced awareness is constantly reinforced by exercising these vows. All the ethic that is needed is contained in them. As a minister abides by them, loves them and cherishes them, by them a spiritual minister sets their course. No other ethic is needed.

The blessing of the infinite spirit is upon you.∞

To be a
Minister
Is a sacred
Trust
Drawing out
The Divine
In Each One
Searching.

LETTER OF CALL
FOR
MINISTERS

*T*he method of creating GOD UNLIMITED churches is to have the minister be a full member of the church board, accompanied by two others agreeable to the minister, and for it to be totally under the minister's direction. Thus all of the blocks to the minister's success are taken away, yet corporate restraints are still there. This is, of course, based on the corporation as presented in this manual for the churches. If a minister needs a call letter, the following may be molded to fit the individual needs. Religious Nonprofit Corporation requirements can vary from state to state and also within California subsequent to publication of the *Ministers Manual*.

*T*he (*name of the church*) of GOD UNLIMITED of (*city and state*) does hereby extend a call to (*minister's name*) to assume the pulpit of this church to serve as its regular Minister beginning (*full date*). It is understood (*minister's name*) will serve this Church as its Ecclesiastical Head and Educational Director.

The specific terms of this call are as follows:

The Church agrees to pay (*minister's name*) remuneration in the amount of (*dollars*) per month or (*percent*) of the gross income of the Church, whichever is greater, payable on the 15th and last day of each month. This remuneration shall be designated as salary, housing allowance, etc, and shall be reviewed at the end of the first six months period with a view to escalation if justified by attendance and budgetary balance.

From the Church operating account the Minister will use a credit card account to maintain his car in gas, repairs and insurance.

Minister will be paid a bonus of ten percent on monthly gross income over $4,000. Gifts to the Minister for counseling or for specific practitioner work is separate income for him.

Gross income to the Church does not include contributions to the building fund or special project funds, but does include all other income.

The salary and benefits to be paid the Minister of this Member Church may be increased from time to time, by the Board of Directors, as it deems appropriate, but shall not be reduced or adversely changed without the prior knowledge and consent of the Minister.

This Church, a MEMBER CHURCH of the Church of God Unlimited, agrees to pay Minister's expenses to official and ecclesiastical gatherings of the church; namely (list events extant).

The Minister of this Church shall conduct accredited classwork as outlined by the Commission on Education of GOD UNLIMITED at its International Headquarters.

It is agreed that the Minister shall be entitled to an annual vacation with pay, for a period of four weeks, and that the Church will be responsible for compensation paid to guest speakers during that period.

It is agreed that the Minister be provided health and accident insurance as recommended by a reliable insurance company to meet reasonable needs, paid for by the Church.

(signed) _____
President of the Board of Directors

(signed) _____
Secretary of the Board of Directors

Date _____

I, (Minister's name) accept the terms and conditions of this Call as outlined in this Letter of Call.

(signed) _____
Minister

The true
Worship service
Dedicates itself
To exaulting
God in each
Of us.

Theme 6

WORSHIP SERVICES

SUNDAY MORNING
ORDER OF WORSHIP
I

Organ Prelude

Opening Meditation and Treatment

Let us enter into the awareness of the inner presence which is God *and in quietness and peace claim our oneness with the Infinite now and forevermore. We say in unison: I AM GOD, GOD I AM!*

Bible Reading

Minister's Prayer

Hymn (as announced)

Remain standing for: *Lord's Prayer*
(Sing It Together)

Congregational Reading

Announcements

Silent Treatment

(Healing Treatment by minister and practitioner for all present, while congregation are in meditation; background organ or piano music.)

INSPIRATIONAL TALK

Meditation followed by congregation singing hymn: *Open My Eyes*

Offering—Piano or Organ Offertory

Doxology Hymn: *Praise God*

Benediction

I love you, I love you, I love you. As you go now into the world you have created with your love, it showers back to you that which you are, perfect peace.

Postlude

II

Organ Prelude

Healing Service

Hymn

Announcements

The Lord's Prayer (Sing It Together)

Meditation Hymn: *Open My Eyes*

INSPIRATIONAL TALK

Offertory Solo

Benediction

Doxology: *Praise God*

Postlude

III

Healing Meditation

Morning Prelude

Hymn

The Lord's Prayer (standing, sing it together)

Responsive Reading

Solo

The Silence

Hymn: *Open My Eyes*

Morning address: INSPIRATIONAL TALK

The Offering

Recognizing God as the source of my supply, I bless and dedicate this offering to the truth which sets man free.

The Blessing

Good closing song:

NOW THERE IS PEACE ON EARTH

Now there is peace on earth,
And it has begun with me.
Now there is peace on earth,
The peace that was meant to be.
I am God the creator,
One with all of my world.
Walking with my creation,
In perfect harmony.

Now there is peace in all,
For this is the moment now.
With every step I take,
I offer my solemn vow.
To take each moment,
And live each moment,
In peace eternally.
Now there is peace on earth,
For it has begun with ME!

Open my eyes, that I may see

C. H. S.

CHAS. H. SCOTT

1. O-pen my eyes, that I may see Glimp-ses of truth Thou hast for me;
2. O-pen my ears, that I may hear Voic-es of truth Thou send-est clear;
3. O-pen my mouth, and let me bear Glad-ly the warm truth ev-'ry-where;

Place in my hands the won-der-ful key That shall un-clasp, and set me free.
And while the wave-notes fall on my ear, Ev-'ry-thing false will dis-ap-pear.
O-pen my heart, and let me pre-pare Love with Thy chil-dren thus to share.

Si-lent-ly now I wait for Thee, Read-y, my God, Thy will to see;

O-pen my {eyes, ears, heart,} il-lum-ine me, Spir-it di-vine!

Praise God that Good is everywhere

MURRAY

DOXOLOGY

GENEVAN PSALTER

Praise God that Good is ev-'ry-where; Praise to the Love we all may share,

The Life that thrills in you and me; Praise to the Truth that sets us free.

HEALING MEDITATIONS

- *My body is the youthful temple of the living God.*

- *I live, move and have my being in the perfection of Infinite Spirit.*

- *My life outpictures God in me for I AM GOD GOD I AM:*

- *I am whole and perfect.*

- *I like me.*

- *I live in my eternally perfect body.*

- *My body is the temple of the living spirit: every organ, action and function of my body is whole and perfect.*

- *I am the pure white light of love surrounded by harmonious beings.*

- *I am the pure white light of love, surrounded by harmonious circumstances.*

- *I am true to myself: I have fun being me.*

- *I am myself and I have fun.*

- *Good goes from me, good comes to me.*

- *I think my thought and the power of the universe vibrates to manifest it.*

- *I am independently wealthy.*

- *I am master of my habit.*

- *I am a positive being and I create all in my world beneficial to me.*

- *My autoimmune system functions perfectly.*

- *I am ingenuous.*

- *My purpose in life is to listen to the divine within.*

- *I am the center of peace.*

- *My body reflects my thought about it.*

- *To the pure all is pure.*

- *I am harmonious with all my creation.*

- *I am an eternally happy being.*

- *I live in my eternally happy body.*

- *I accede to my spritual plan.*

- *My skin is pure and supple.*

- *My body is lithe and youthful.*

- *I live in my inner peace.*

- *I am harmonious with all my creation.*

- *I am at peace.*

- *I am exonerated of past thought, word and action: I live in my pure now.*

- *To know truth is to know existence: to LIVE truth is to enjoy in practice its fruits.*

- *I am my attitude about life.*

- *To the pure all is pure.*

- *I think my thought and the power of the universe vibrates to manifest it.*

- *I am my attitude about me.*

- *I have unlimited financial stability.*

This Place is . . .
The
Home of God.

Maekawa Miki, Shinto Prophetess

A GOD UNLIMITED CHURCH DEDICATION SERVICE

*W*henever a church is established in the GOD UNLIMITED family of churches, upon affiliation, a representative from International Headquarters participates as founder in the church dedication.

Affirmation Before
The Congregation

MINISTER: We dedicate this church to the eternal light of God that lighteth everyman's journey through life.

FOUNDER: We dedicate this church to the light of God as man, in which light we walk.

MINISTER: We dedicate this church to the one life which is over all, in all, and through all.

FOUNDER: We dedicate this church to the life of God as man, the one Life, that life is our life now.

MINISTER: We dedicate this church to the limitless love of God and to the givingness of divine spirit.

FOUNDER: We dedicate this church to the love of God as man, embracing all humanity.

MINISTER: We dedicate this church to the Law as good that governs all things.

FOUNDER: We dedicate this church to those who use this Law of cause and effect as good knowing it meets the needs of all who enter into this *healing temple.*

MINISTER: We dedicate this church to the peace of God indwelling that passeth all understanding.

FOUNDER: We dedicate this church to the contemplation of that peace knowing it dwells in the hearts, minds and souls of all who enter here.

MINISTER: We dedicate this church to the unerring guidance of the all-knowing spirit.

FOUNDER: We dedicate this church to the intuition of man that perceives this guidance and is directed by it.

MINISTER: We dedicate this church to the eternal wholeness and unity of all life.

FOUNDER: We dedicate this church to the wholeness of the divine man as God knowing he accepts that wholeness here and now.

MINISTER: We dedicate this church to the worship of God in spirit and in truth.

FOUNDER: We dedicate this church to the mystical union of God as man.

MINISTER: We dedicate this church to the eternal father and the everlasting mother of all creation.

FOUNDER: We dedicate this church to the loving presence as the eternal son, the Christ inborn within us.

MINISTER: We dedicate this church to the Healing Presence.

FOUNDER: We dedicate this church to the acceptance of this healing presence by all who enter here.

MINISTER: We dedicate this church to the everlasting divine imagination that creates all things.

FOUNDER: We dedicate this church to the intuition in man perceiving all things.

MINISTER: We dedicate this church to the laughter of God.

FOUNDER: We dedicate this church to the joy of man.

MINISTER: We dedicate this church to infinite beauty.

FOUNDER: We dedicate this church to that which is beautiful in all things and in all people.

MINISTER: We dedicate this church to the divine abundance, in all humanity.

FOUNDER: We dedicate this church to the fulfillment of every good and perfect desire.

MINISTER: We dedicate this church to the birthless and deathless God.

FOUNDER: We dedicate this church to the life of man, eternal and ever expanding.

MINISTER: We dedicate this church to communion with God.

FOUNDER: We dedicate this church to communion with our fellowman through the divine in all people.

Benediction

MINISTER: And now the spirit of peace abides with you.

FOUNDER: The life of the spirit flows through each of you.

MINISTER: The eternal light of God goes before each of you.

FOUNDER: This light directs your pathways.

MINISTER: The love of God now enfolds you.

FOUNDER: The power of God upholds you always.

MINISTER: THIS CHURCH IS BLESSED!!!

FOUNDER: THIS CHURCH BLESSES ALL WHO ENTER!

MINISTER: THIS CHURCH IS PROSPERED.

FOUNDER: ALL WHO ENTER HERE ARE PROSPERED.

MINISTER: The original purity and integrity of every man abides in this church.

FOUNDER: This reality heals all who enter here.

MINISTER: The indwelling lord bless thee and keep thee.

FOUNDER: The light of heaven guides each of you on your path as each of you experience divine wholeness NOW!   AMEN!

MINISTER and FOUNDER: *AND SO IT IS!*

RECEPTION
OF NEW MEMBERS

*T*he order of service for receiving new members into a Church of God Unlimited:

The minister says:

One of the most satisfying of human experiences is to be aware of man's deliberate effort toward selfunfoldment, thereby making it possible for more of the Divine potential to express through him. In furthering this effort, we have chosen to unify ourselves—with high purpose and love—in membership in our church.

This is not the church and its members—this is the church as its members. The body of the church is composed of individuals who are its hands, its feet, its head and its heart.

Within the body of the church moves the spirit of the church. You have deliberately made yourselves an integral part of this movement. Every individual is an individualization of the presence of God. The presence of God is the divine spirit which is God. Through each other, and in our unified awareness, we share our experience of the presence of God. And each time we think of the spirit of our church, we attune ourselves with the sum of the power, the life and the love, which is the "Healing Presence" that indwells the body of our church.

GOD UNLIMITED teaches the philosophy of the technique or science of how man deliberately cooperates with the divine nature of God, the expression of which is the will of God for man. It is the Ministry of Healing, the purpose of which is to reveal the inherent divinity—the wholeness of spirit within man, to heal man's sense of separation from his own source. Healing is not just of the body, but to make whole means to return to our original purity and integrity, to be true to ourself and have fun living a dynamically wholesome abundant life. In short, GOD UNLIMITED is a teaching by which life is "raised" to the joy level, and established there.

We believe that the creative process is the Healing Presence within each individual; and as authority for that belief, there are among us those who have been healed in body, mind and affairs Thus, from our own "fruits" do we take "our" authority.

There are among us at this time those who have signified their desire to become members of this church. I now present (the chairman of the Board of Directors or a board officer, by name) who will *officially welcome our new members.*

The welcoming official says:

You are unifying with each other and with the members of this church and of all member churches of GOD UNLIMITED *throughout the world, in a warm, loving, divine fellowship of the spirit. As you enter into this church activity in thought, word, purpose, plan and action, you are important in a unique way to each other and to all humanity. Through your adherence to, and practice of, the teachings of* GOD UNLIMITED *as taught by the University of Healing, you become a vital factor in establishing and maintaining the kingdom of heaven in everyman.*

As you join in membership cooperation, the experience of each is enlarged and expanded into greater good, for as you enter into a life of service to mankind, to life itself, as God, you knowingly become one with the very spirit of the divine presence, which you are. In this way you increasingly become an influence for good in the lives of all whom you contact, but mostly, in the revelation of the divine within yourself.

The one obligation placed upon you is the obligation you place on yourself in the fulfillment of the purpose in your heart and the meaning of this membership to you.

You have agreed to unfold the divinity within to its highest and greatest potential. Your only solemn pledge is to God in yourself and to God as yourself.

On behalf of our Board of Directors and the congregational members of this church, I lovingly receive each of you into this unique purely spiritual

147

relationship as members of the Church of God Un-limited: (Name Church include in its articles of incorporation.)

Congregation, I joyously present to you the following new members of the (Name) *church:*

Mr/Mrs/(youngsters, full name)*/etc.*

(Chairman shakes hands with each one and begins applause.)

Yes, and
A
Little
Child
Shall
Lead them.

God blessed them.
And God said unto them,
Be fruitful
And multiply
And replenish
The earth . . .
And it was so.

Genesis 1:28:30

Theme 7

BAPTISMS
WEDDINGS

BAPTISM SERVICE
FOR CHILDREN

*T*he rite of baptism is a recognition of the loving presence and infinite power of the spirit, which is God, in each child. The seed of perfection is implanted in every child and awaits only the baptism of spirit, the outpouring of truth, for the complete recognition of good in his life.

The christening ceremony can be called by several names including: Naming Ceremony, where the child or person is called by the name selected by the family; Christening Ceremony, where the parents are dedicating themselves to raise their children in the traditions and the values which they hold dear; and, Baptism Ceremony, where the person involved is old enough to present themself to be recognized by their name before their religious peers.

And they brought unto him also infants that he would touch them: but when his disciples saw it, they rebuked them. But Jesus called them unto him, and said, Suffer little children to come unto me, and forbid them not: for of such is the kingdom of God. And he took them up in his arms and put his hands upon them and blessed them.[1]

Members of the congregation of God Unlimited:

This consecration service welcomes into our fellowship the (infant) (daughter) (son) (son daughter children) of (name of family).

It is an outward ritual intended to reveal an inward unity of spirit.

(At this point, the minister steps down to where the parents are waiting having been previously called forward, the father holding the child.)

We recognize that a child comes forth from God, as God, a divine creation, and that the heavenly father's perfection is the very being, the life of this child. A Godly purity and goodness is incarnate in the child, as its own life. Baptism symbol-

---

[1]   Luke 18:15 [KJV]

izes our recognition of the immersion of the human in the Divine Life Stream, our oneness as God. It symbolizes our faith that this being on its new adventure must live and move and have its existence within the consciousness of God, and will always be in an all-embracing circle of divine love and so . . . (Husband's first name) *and* (wife's first name):

In presenting (this child/these children) for (spiritual baptism/christening) you are to be convinced in your own mind that you are immersed in the spirit of God, and God is in you as you, so acknowledging the divine oneness of spirit, soul and body, one universal truth which is the same on every plane. You believe that man is a creative expression or experience of God and is God.

You realize that keeping the mind set on good leads to joy and accomplishment in life. Teach your child the truth of being, that from childhood (he/she/they) may realize (his/her/their) unity with God and as God, and all that this implies? Conduct your own lives so that not only by word, but by example (he/she/they) may learn to live joyously, creatively and harmoniously with divine principle? Do this to the best of your ability.

(They reply): WE WILL

(Charge the godparents, at this point, if there are any, they will have come forward with the parents, standing to the rear of them:)

As the godparents of (this child/these dren) you are charged with faithfulness to the ideals stated in the charge to the parents and with the responsibility of seeing to the spiritual welfare of (this child these children) should need arise and it become you to stand in the place of friend and counselor.

(Minister takes child in his arms, if he wishes. He addresses god-parents, if present, and parents)

What name shall be given to this child?

(And then, repeating the name given, he shall baptize the child/or children, saying):

I (Christen you /name/ and baptize you) in the name of the father, and of the son, and of the holy spirit. The father in whom you live, the son, the Christ within you, and the holy spirit, the moving creative principle of all life, your very God nature.

(Prayer)

I dedicate (this child/these children) to the end that perfect intelligence guides and directs (him/her/them) and unfailing love draws (him/her/them) into the ways of eternal happiness.
AMEN

or)

This child now comes to know that as (he/she/they) is/are now enfold in my arms, so always is/are (he/she/they) enfolded in strength and awareness of (his/her/their) divine heritage. As God, this child is absolutely perfect right now (add above prayer.)   AND SO IT IS.

ADULT BAPTISM SERVICE

*P*reamble may be taken from preceding baptism service. Then the following may be used:

In presenting yourself for baptism, you acknowledge your faith in the oneness of God as man. You further acknowledge your faith not only in your unity with the indwelling Christ, but also that this act places a seal upon that union.

Believe that you are immersed in the Spirit of God as God; that in him you live and move and have your being. Conduct your life in harmony with this truth of being.

ANSWER: I WILL!

Prayer invoking blessing of the Holy Spirit:

Minister (using water, rose petals, or whatever substance is significant for this service) states:

I baptize you in the name of the father and of the son and of the holy spirit; the father in whom you live, the son, the Christ within you; the holy spirit the moving creative principle of all life, your very God nature.   AMEN

Have you not read that
He who made them
At the beginning
Made them male and female.
For this reason
A man shall leave
his father and mother
And be joined to his wife,
And the two
Shall become one.

Matthew 19:4-6

Create your own wedding

WEDDING CEREMONY
ONE

*W*e are assembled here in the presence of God and these friends to celebrate the joining of this man and this woman in the unity of marriage.

In a moment of silence, we blend our consciousness in the gladness on this occasion.

(To the bride and groom.)

There are no obligations on earth more sweet or tender than those you are about to assume. There are no vows more solemn than those you are about to make. There is no human institution more sacred than that of the home you are about to form.

True marriage is the holiest of all earthly relationships. It should be entered into reverently, thoughtfully and with full understanding of its sacred nature. Marriage to be complete must first be spiritual. From this inner state of conscious unity in faith, love, thought, purpose, plan and action, there comes the outer state corresponding to it, making the outer, like the inner, peaceful and harmonious.

The spiritual marriage provides for an ever upward progression of the individual being. The creative spirit is allowed to prevail in thought, word and deed.

The life of your marriage is the beholding of each other as an expression of God.

Love moves each being to a fuller development. The pure motive of giving greater enjoyment of life is LOVE in your union.

The light of understanding of boundless experiences yet to be is consciously nurtured in a spiritual union.

The state of matrimony is true marriage only when based upon this deep, invisible union of two beings who find reflection in one another.

Do you understand this?

(The persons to be married shall answer): I DO!

Power abides and proceeds from this unity. This action promotes health, wealth and happiness. Peace and harmony are then secure in the wholesomeness of this home. Beauty abounds as each aspect of living is properly proportioned.

Material, physical, mental, emotional and spiritual expression finds perfect balance through each of you.

Joy reigns as your separate lives merge into one. Self expression is a stepping stone to something more excellent enfolding you in the faith and love of God.

Will you bring to this sharing, each for the sake of the other, the best that you have in you? Do each of you seek to express your life together at the highest level of understanding?

(The persons to be married shall answer): I DO!

Who presents this woman to be married to this man?

(The father or mother of the bride or whoever gives her in marriage shall answer): I DO! (or) WE DO! (or) HER MOTHER AND I DO!

Will you please join hands.

(Then the minister shall cause the man with his right hand to take the woman by her right hand and say after him):

(First name of the groom) will you take this woman, whose hand you hold, choosing her alone to be your wedded wife? Will you live with her in the true state of matrimony? Will you love her, comfort her, honor her at all times and be faithful to her?

(The man will answer) I WILL!

(First name of the bride) will you take this man, whose hand you hold, to be your wedded husband? Will you live with him, comfort him, honor him at all times and be faithful to him?

(The woman will answer) I WILL!

(The minister shall cause the man with his right hand to take the woman by her right hand and say after him):

I (groom's first name) TAKE YOU, (bride's first name) TO BE MY WEDDED WIFE; TO LOVE AND CHERISH FROM THIS DAY FORWARD; AND THERETO I PLEDGE YOU MY FAITH.

(Then the minister shall have the bride repeat after him):

I (bride's first name) TAKE YOU (groom's first name) TO BE MY WEDDED HUSBAND; TO LOVE AND CHERISH FROM THIS DAY FORWARD; AND THERETO I PLEDGE YOU MY FAITH.

What token do you give of your sincerity?

(Then they shall loose hands and the best man shall hand the ring to the minister. The bride will give her flowers to the maid of honor.)

This ring is blessed and he who gives it and she who wears it do abide in the peace and love of God, living together in unity, in love and in happiness, and with good purpose for a happy life. **AMEN**

This ring is the symbol of the unbroken unity of truth now to be symbolized in your married life.

(The minister shall then deliver the ring to the man to put upon the third finger of the woman's left hand. The man, holding the ring there, shall say after the minister:)

Please repeat after me.

WITH THIS RING, I (groom's first name), THEE WED. LET IT EVER BE TO US A SYMBOL OF ETERNAL LOVE, AS A TOKEN OF OUR FAITHFULNESS, EACH TO THE OTHER, I PLACE IT NOW ON YOUR HAND.

(As the man continues to hold the ring upon her finger, the bride will repeat after the minister)

AS A TOKEN OF OUR FAITHFULNESS, EACH TO THE OTHER, I (bride's first name), GIVE IT PLACE UPON MY HAND.

(In a double ring ceremony, the minister shall ask the bride)

What token do you give of your sincerity?

(Matron hands the ring to the minister)

BLESS, oh God, this ring, that she who gives it and he who wears it may ever abide in peace and love of God, living together in unity, in love and in happiness and with good purpose for a happy life. **AMEN**

This ring is a symbol of the unbroken truth now to be symbolized in your married life.

(The minister shall deliver the ring to the woman to put upon the third finger of the man's left hand and the woman, holding the ring there, she shall say after the minister:)

LET THIS RING EVER BE TO US A SYMBOL OF OUR LOVE. AS A TOKEN OF OUR FAITHFULNESS EACH TO THE OTHER, I PLACE IT NOW UPON YOUR HAND.

(As the woman continues to hold the ring upon the groom's hand, the man will repeat after the minister:)

AS A TOKEN OF OUR FAITHFULNESS, EACH TO THE OTHER, I GIVE IT PLACE UPON MY HAND.

(Then the minister shall say)

I now speak to you of marriage:

Heavenly Marriage

Marriage is a magic state
Created out of infinite cosmos
Bringing together two beings
Who find honor and joy in each other.

Marriage first is the natural
Symbiosis of two souls
Whose great delight
Excels in each others presence.

Marriage is the recognition
One's self in another
But honors
Uniqueness in each.

Each soul, married or not,
Has its indwelling purpose
Has its special charisma
Which will always be free.

The magic of spiritual marriage
Is its continual recognition
That each unfold and expand
Or the light within is stifled.

The marriage made in heaven
creates both eternally free
And delights in individuality
Immortally aflame in its own magic.

Herbert L Beierle

LET US PRAY

Eternal spirit, life, truth and substance of all, we now feel a conscious unity with you. We joy in this awareness. We know that this man and this woman, who have entered into this spiritual union are forever conscious of your indwelling presence. They are one with each other as they are ever one with you. They rejoice in perfect love and perfect peace together and live in accord with the true Law of their divine being. **AMEN**

In as much as you, (groom's full name), and you, (bride's full name), have consented together in bonds of wedlock and have witnessed the same before God and these present and have pledged your faith each to the other, I now pronounce you husband and wife, to live in harmony with God's love ever one with you!

(Minister's closing prayer)

In the name of the father, this union is blessed with enduring happiness, with peace, love and prosperity through all the years to come.
AMEN

(Couple Kiss and Turn)

IT IS MY GOOD PLEASURE TO PRESENT TO YOU MR AND MRS (husband's first and last name).

WEDDING
GUEST
AFFIRMATION

To be read and said by those
present about the couple

I, friend of (groom) and (bride)
Do bless this marriage.

I feel the sacredness
Of their stated principles
For successful living.

I happily support these ideals.

I give my thought, word and deed
In support of their lives.

It is my joy to sustain them
With my friendship and love.

I accept their friendship to me.

I bless this event as very good.

AND SO IT IS!

WEDDING CEREMONY TWO

Minister:

*W*e come at this hour to celebrate the convergence of two lives, those of (groom's first name) and (bride's first name), in the unity of marriage.

True marriage is the holiest of all earthly relationships. It should be entered into thoughtfully, and with full understanding of its sacred nature. Marriage to be complete must first be spiritual. From this inner state of conscious unity in faith, love, thought, purpose, plan and action, there comes the outer, like the inner, peaceful and harmonious.

The spiritual marriage is the beholding of each other as an expression of God.

Love moves each being to a fuller development. The pure motive of giving greater enjoyment of life is LOVE in your union.

The light of understanding of boundless experiences yet to be is consciously nurtured in a spiritual union.

The state of matrimony is true marriage only when based upon this deep, invisible union of two beings who find reflection in one another. Do you understand this?

Couple say: YES. WE DO.

Minister: Of all the men and women you know, you have chosen each other as partners in your life's journey together. Are you ready to be married?

Couple say: WE ARE!

Minister: (Parents of the Bride and Parents of the Groom) are you willing, now and always, to support and strengthen this marriage by upholding (bride) and (groom) with your love and concern?

Parents say: YES, WE ARE!

Minister: Let us share these words on marriage—

You were born again to be together again unto eternity—Within the Wings of Cosmic Oneness.—In your togetherness though let there be freedom and space—To dance the Dance of Life without restraint.— —Love deeply but not possessively—Like the ripples on the water—Let it flow between you—

*Serve each other but become not a servant.— —
Share, but share alike; be joyous and gay together—But find time for solitude.—Find time to be
alone—Like the keys upon a harpsichord, separate
and alone,—But together they give forth heavenly
music.— —Let being speak to being—Let there be a
mutual interchange—But not forevermore—For only
Life itself can claim—The right as keeper of the
being.— —Walk together—But like the trees—
Within the woods,—Leave room between—to light
your way.*

(Groom) and (Bride), would you now drink to
one another. Fill each other's cup, but drink from
your own. Let this act signalize your promise to
one another to be yourselves and to risk what you
are for the sake of what you yet can be.

(Couple pour the wine and drink to one another.)

(Bride): (Groom), I take you in all your gentle-
ness and warmth to be my husband and compan-
ion, my lover and best friend. I want to love you
for yourself in the knowledge that you will become
all that you can be. I want you with me for all the
days of my life to share whatever life may bring us.

(Groom): (Bride), your love and wisdom has
shown me many paths to truth and beauty. I want
you to be my mate forever.

(Bride takes ring from bridesmaid, groom
takes ring from best man.)

(Bride): With this exchange of rings we express
to family and friends our shared knowledge that
we will continue exploring the exchange we have
come to love over the past years.

(Groom): We shall not cease our exploration and the end of all our exploring will be to arrive where we started and know the place for the first time.

Minister: (Groom and Bride), by doing so and speaking your vows before this loving company, you have pronounced yourselves husband and wife. We who are present and those not here who care, know that the inspiration of this moment will not be forgotten. As your affection for each other has always a little more to grow, so it will rise from you and enter into the lives of others. Let us remember, love does not consist of gazing into each other's eyes, but in looking together in the same direction.

WEDDING CEREMONY THREE

(Groom on left of minister)

Minister:

*W*e are gathered here this day to listen to the promises of (Groom) and (Bride) as they begin a new life together. These two people have entered into a total commitment to each other, yet with the understanding that in marriage it is important to remain individuals, for only in this way will the marriage prosper. They wish to follow the ideals expressed here:

M

You were born again
To be together again
Unto Eternity
Within the Wings
Of Cosmic Oneness.

A

In your togetherness, though
Let there be
Freedom and space
To dance the Dance of Life
Without restraint.

R

Love deeply but not possessively
Like the ripples on the water
Let it flow between you
Serve each other
But become not a servant.

R

Share,
But share alike;
Be joyous and gay together
But find time for solitude.
Find time to be alone.

I

Like the keys
Upon a harpsichord,
Separate and alone
But together
they give forth heavenly music.

A

Let being speak to being
Let there be a mutual interchange
But not forever more
For only Life itself can claim
The right as keeper of the beingness.

G

Walk together
But like the trees
Within the woods
Leave room between
To light your way.

E

Minister: These promises that you make today must be made again tomorrow and renewed each day.

(Groom): I promise you the love that I am. I offer you all the happiness I can give. In the knowledge that together we can achieve a union greater than the sum of its parts.

(Bride): I offer you the best of what I am, and the best of what I will be. I ask only for the opportunity to share the joy of our future closeness.

Minister: There are no obligations on earth more sweet and tender than those you are about to assume. There are no vows more solemn than those you are about to make. There is no human institution more sacred than that of the home you are about to form.

True marriage is the holiest of all earthly relationships. It should be entered into reverently, thoughtfully and with full understanding of its sacred nature. Marriage to be complete must first be spiritual. From this inner state of conscious unity in faith, love, thought, purpose, plan and action, there comes the outer state corresponding to it, making the outer like the inner, peaceful and harmonious.

The spiritual marriage provides for an ever upward progression of the individual being. The creative spirit is allowed to prevail in thought, word and deed.

The life of your marriage is the beholding of each other as an expression of God.

Love moves each soul to a fuller development. The pure motive of giving greater enjoyment of life is LOVE in your union.

The light of understanding of boundless experiences yet to be is consciously nurtured in a spiritual union.

The state of matrimony is true marriage only when based upon this deep, invisible union of two beings who seek to find completion in one another. Do you understand this?

(Bride and Groom answer): I DO!

Power abides and proceeds from this unity. This action promotes health, wealth and happiness. Peace and harmony are then secure in the wholesomeness of this home. Beauty abounds as each aspect of living is properly proportioned.

Material, physical, mental, emotional and spiritual expression finds perfect balance through each of you.

Joy reigns as your separate lives merge into one. Self expression is a stepping stone to something more excellent, enfolding you in the faith and love of God.

Will you bring to this new life, each for the sake of the other, the best that you have in you? Do each of you seek to express your life together at the highest level of understanding?

(Groom and Bride answer): I DO!

Minister: (Groom), this token of your sincerity, this ring, is a symbol of unbroken unity—the unity of Truth, now to be displayed in your married life.

(Groom): (Bride), will you take this and wear this ring as a symbol of our love and our life together?

(Bride): I WILL!

(Bride): (Groom), will you take and wear this ring as a symbol of our love and our life together?

(Groom): I WILL!

IN AS MUCH AS you, (Groom), and you (Bride), have consented together in bonds of wedlock and have witnessed the same before God and these present and have pledged your faith each to the other, I now pronounce you husband and wife, to live in harmony with God's LOVE ever ONE with you.

Let us pray: In the name of the Father, this union is blessed with enduring happiness, with peace, love and prosperity through all the years to come.
AMEN

It is my good pleasure to present to you, Mr and Mrs (groom's full name). ∞

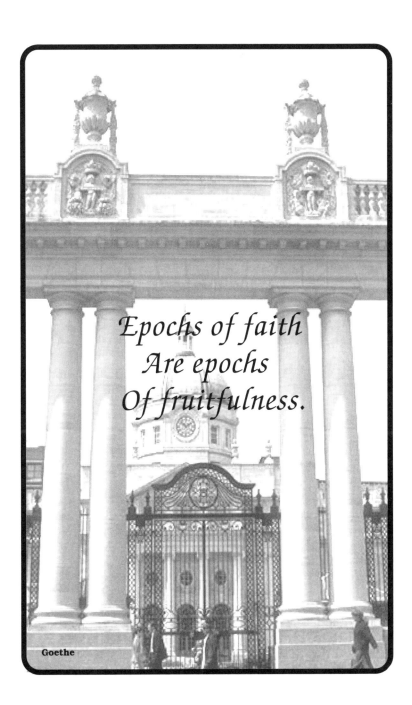

Epochs of faith
Are epochs
Of fruitfulness.

Goethe

FIFTIETH
WEDDING ANNIVERSARY
CEREMONY

*W*e are gathered here in the sight of God and in the presence of each other to bless (groom) and (bride) as they renew the sacred vows which they took fifty years ago.

True marriage is the result of two beings coming together in that union which is the most sacred of all earthly unions. There are no ties on Earth so sweet and tender as those you assumed fifty years ago. There is no institution on Earth so sacred as that of the home you formed.

Your separate lives with their own memories, joys, expectations, opportunities and experiences, were merged in one on that wonderful day.

(Groom), you took (bride) to be your wife, to love her, comfort her, honor and cherish her at all times and to cling to her alone. (Bride), you took (groom) to be your true husband, to love him, to honor him and cherish him at all times and to cling to him alone.

(Groom) you placed a wedding ring on (bride)'s finger, a symbol of the unbroken unity of married life. You placed it on her finger as a token of faithfulness each to the other, and she gave it place upon her hand as a token of faithfulness one to the other.

You consented together in the holy bonds of wedlock and were pronounced man and wife in the name of the eternal father and the eternal mother of all creation.

On that momentous day, perhaps you were thinking of your own happiness. As the years have passed, the happiness of many others have been involved with yours. Through these fifty years, the happiness you had on that day has shed its beam of light on all whom you have known or contacted. There have been many challenges to patience and wisdom. Your love has met them all, for it is wise and understanding, as well as warm and strong. You performed an act of faith, believing in each other to the utmost. That faith has been honored. Through the years you have been unmoved in your devotion. You always remained confident and sure.

After fifty years of married life you stand in our presence, bearing witness to the fact that two beings have the power to love each other more and more, indefinitely; that the larger the love becomes, the more lovable do the objects of that love become; and that the consciousness of perfect unity in pure affection increases constantly as those two beings find their oneness with God. You stand in our presence as an inspiration to each one who has entered into the bonds of holy matrimony, and we all ask that at the end of fifty years we may stand in the presence of others with the same grace, beauty and strength, and bear witness to the power of love.

And now, on this happy day, you are renewing your covenant of love, loyalty and devotion to each other. And even as God blessed your marriage fifty years ago, we know that God as you blesses this renewal of covenants.

In the awareness of the indwelling God, which has led you in the midst of joy and difficulty, in the presence of your children, grandchildren and friends, you are again performing an act of faith, believing in each other to the utmost as you give to each other your heart and your hand all that you have and all that you are.

(Join your right hands.)

(Groom), fifty years ago you pledged your troth to (bride), and took her to be your wedded wife. These fifty years have found you faithful to your pledge. Will you, therefore, now at the close of this half century, in the awareness of God indwelling, in the presence of your children, in the presence of your grandchildren and in the presence of these friends who have gathered here, renew your vows of love and loyalty, and continue this devotion to her so long as you both shall live? Will you thus renew your spiritual unity?

(Groom): I WILL!

(Bride), fifty years ago you pledged your troth to (groom), and you took him to be your wedded husband. These fifty years have found you faithful to your pledge. Will you therefore, now at the close of this half century, in the awareness of the indwelling God, in the presence of your children, in the presence of your grandchildren, and in the presence of these friends who have gathered here, renew your vows of love and of loyalty, and continue this devotion to him as long as you both shall live? Will you thus renew your spiritual unity?

(Bride): I WILL!

God's blessing is upon you!

(Short Prayer by Minister).

Live near to God
And all things
Will appear
Little to you
In comparison
With eternal realities.

Robert McCheyne

Theme 8

SPECIAL SERVICES

GOOD FRIDAY SERVICE

*T*he Good Friday Service, is in many GOD UNLIM-
ITED churches used as a specific healing experience. Requests for treatment are accepted and
treatments given by the minister and students. In
a small church, the Good Friday Service can be
presented by the minister alone, following the
same "order of service" for each period.

The Good Friday Service can be seen as a time
of meditation, and instead of treatment work, silent meditation is highlighted.

The three-period program features an address
given in each period. In the first period, the subject

might be "Ministry of Jesus" or "The Background Life of Jesus."

The second address would then be "The Crucifixion Experience and Its Inner Meaning" or "The Seven Last Words."

The address for the last period could concern "The Eternal Christ" or "The Persistent Ministry of the Triumph."

A different speaker could be used for each period if it is desired.

Further ideas for a three-period series of talks are: **The Trial, The Tomb, The Triumph**. Another good short-title connected series: **The Preparation, The Ministry, The Victory**; all from the metaphysical viewpoint.

ORDER OF SERVICE

A typical three-period service:

FIRST HOUR

> **Meditation Music**
>
> **Introduction: The Minister**
>
> **Treatment: Student**
>
> **Song**
>
> **Lesson: *THE CHRIST IDEA***
>
> **Meditation**
>
> **Meditation Hymn**
>
> **Closing Treatment: The Minister**

SECOND HOUR

> **Meditation Music**
>
> **Introduction: The Minister**
>
> **Treatment: Student**
>
> **Song**
>
> **Lesson: *THE STORY ITSELF***
>
> **Meditation Hymn**
>
> **Closing Treatment: The Minister**

THIRD HOUR

Meditation Music

Introduction: The Minister

Treatment: Student

Song

Lesson: *THE SEVEN LAST WORDS*

Meditation

Meditation Hymn

Closing Treatment: The Minister

A simple order of service each hour:

Music

Introduction

Meditation

Message

Music

MEDITATION AND THEMES

*P*alm Sunday is the spirit in the race of man yearning for expression, security and joy. Hailing the Christ, we enter into that joy.

Good Friday is Adam-man made blind by his own needless fears, putting himself into a tomb. Denying the Christ we enter the tomb.

Easter is the son of God, Christ-man, in everyman, waking and rising into light, leaving all darkness forever. Accepting the Christ we enter into that light.

KEY IDEAS

Good Friday is what had to happen for Easter to take place.

The gift of the Christ.

Our service is one of meditation for the purpose of our giving LOVE to the world. The background of this occasion is prayer.

This service is a "vigil" of prayer—an ancient mystic tradition. This service is a healing service where, in the name of the indwelling Christ, we speak our word for those asking treatment.

THE SEVEN LAST WORDS

Bible references: Luke 22:32-38; Luke 23:39-43; John 19:25-27; Mark 15:33-37; John 19:28-29, 30; Luke 23:44-49.

FATHER, FORGIVE THEM; FOR THEY KNOW NOT WHAT THEY DO.

TODAY SHALT THOU BE WITH ME IN PARADISE.

WOMAN, BEHOLD THY SON! (SON) BEHOLD THY MOTHER.

MY GOD, MY GOD, FOR THIS WAS I PREPARED.[1]

I THIRST.

IT IS FINISHED.

FATHER, INTO THY HANDS I COMMEND MY SPIRIT. ∞

---

[1]   Lamsa

A time of silence
Is a joyous inward journey
Into total oneness.

It is a time
Of loving awareness
Of the indwelling presence.

Purely revealing itself
As us in us through us
Perfectly now.

Silence is a time
Of peaceful awareness
Of who and what we are.

The full realization
that:
I am God, God I am!

THE SILENCE

*M*inisters and leaders are sometimes less than effective as they conduct prayers or a silence before an audience. They forget that it is **for the audience** that they are conducting the silence and prayer service.

It is necessary for the ministers and practitioners to create a meaningful service. This is done first by recognizing that we lead the silence for others. Too often we withdraw and turn our thoughts and words inward. At all times while the platform we project outward.

Clear speaking is spiritual communication, be articulate. To speak quietly and still be heard requires great awareness and practice. (sotto voce)

When leading a silence or prayer treatment, use short clear statements. The treatment may be new to some listeners. If a phrase is fumbled, go back over it again to insure that it gets across.

Repeat each statement several times in the same way in the process of explaining it. This will allow the listener to become familiar with it before asking them to repeat the statement with us.

Use the phrasing and emphasis desired of the audience, if we want certain words to be emphasized, we emphasize them.

As we speak reverently, never flippantly, of things that deserve reverence, our audience will be reverent of the truth also.

When leading a group be definite. Let them know when we want them to repeat a statement with us by saying: "Together please!" Stress the first word, prolonging it slightly so that the audience will have time to start with us. Help them to cooperate with us, they want to.

Time the repetitious statements. If we want the audience to speak a statement silently so they will then repeat it aloud, make sure they have time to do so.

Do not use the time of silence to preach a sermon. After repeating the statement, give the people time for silent meditation. ∞

CHRISTMAS CANDLELIGHT SERVICE

SIMPLE ORDER OF SERVICE

Prelude
Christmas music

Bible Story
Matthew 2:1-15, Luke 2:1-20

Song
Silent Night

Greeting by Minister

(continued)

Remarks on symbology, its place in religious life, and the particular symbology of the candles of service (see below)

Candle lighting by Congregation
(see below)

Lesson
THE MYSTIC CHRIST

Congregational Song
Oh Come All Ye Faithful

Love Offering

Benediction

ELABORATE SERVICE

Music Prelude

Song
Oh Little Town of Bethlehem

Greetings by Minister
(with preliminary Christmas Message
and basic explanation
of candle lighting)
(see below)

Meditation by student

Minister
explains already-lit candles
(see below)

Trinity Candles
lighted by student who
also explains meanings
(Or can light them
while minister explains)

Song
Joy to the World

Apostolic Candles
Lighted by student with
minister giving explanation.
(Minister must handle this
—it is the crux of the service—
though student
should do the lighting of candles.)

Treatment

(continued)

> ## Candle Lighting
> ## by congregation
> ## (see below)
>
> ## See also notes on pilgrimage idea which can be used at this point.
>
> ## Brief closing meditation.
> ## Congregation to depart in silence.

Notes:

The charm of a Christmas Candlelight Service lies as much in the pageantry of it as in the message it teaches. Each is equally important. The arrangements of candles in the room, auxiliary candles, candles in various parts of the room, if possible, the handling of the musical part of the service, the ease with which the whole thing is presented—due to careful rehearsal—all these are extremely important for this type of service.

The basic set-up includes the following:

One White Candle already lighted before the service, representing Christ spirit.

Three Candles: green, blue and yellow, representing the Trinity. Blue (mind), yellow (spirit), green (body).

Twelve smaller white candles representing the 12 apostles (see meaning).

As many tiny "birthday cake" candles as are needed for expected attendance.

One or more flat dishes, pan-type, with a bed of salt. Use real salt—it is in this bed of salt that the congregation places individually lit candles.

NOTES ON PRESENTATION OF THE CHRISTMAS SERVICE ITSELF

- **PRELIMINARY**

*T*he famous Fra Giovanni letter makes a good beginning item in the greeting. Leader then stresses:

- Something in everyman makes him seek perfection;

- Saviors are people who show us a way;

- The Christchild in each is the spirit of truth, and each must individually give birth to his own recognition of it. It is to symbolize this that we meet this evening.

Bible quotation to begin explanation of candles: Proverbs 20:27—"The Spirit of man is the candle of the Lord."[2] (See E. V. Ingraham on idea of "radiance," "Angel of His Presence" idea, "light of your life" or "aura or halo" ideas.)

With regard to symbols as such: It is the universal language, because symbols make cosmic ideas visible to the individual, without need for words. All spoken language is arbitrary. The mystic seeks a silent truth. Symbology persists because there can be no quarrel with it, as there is with dogmas, doctrine and theology.

The living quality of a flame is a natural symbol of spirit, because it is so clearly something more than the physical form it leaps from. The candle represents spirit in action, burning as the outward sign of the inward life.

---

2   Proverbs 20:27—The spirit of man is the candle of the Lord, searching all the inward part of the belly!

- **APOSTOLIC CANDLES**

*K*ey Ideas: Just as Christ drew unto spirit for his ministry, the men who would put forward that ministry in the world, and the men who could respond to his love, so much each of us call into our life the twelve virtues which we need for support in the ministry of our individual living, for the sake of the spirit indwelling us. Tonight we will take each of the Apostles to symbolize a virtue which we must develop, and we will light them one by one. As we light and explain each one in turn, let each of us examine our own heart to see if this virtue is there.

Peter	FAITH
Andrew	STRENGTH
James, Son of Zebedee	JUDGMENT
John	LOVE
Thomas	UNDERSTANDING
Matthew	WILL
James, Son of Alphaeus	ORDER
Thaddaeus	RENUNCIATION
Philip	POWER
Bartholomew	IMAGINATION
Simon the Canaanite	ZEAL
Judas	LIFE

(The minister will have to do his own thinking at this point: There can be a really tremendous build-up of consciousness during these next few minutes, if the minister will speak with inspiration and power of each of these virtues, but remembering to speak briefly, and not overdo the individual points. Give only the list of Apostles with their corresponding "virtues.")

• A CHRISTMAS MEDITATION

*T*oday I unveil the meaning of the universal Christ within, the son begotten of the only father. In the story of the birth of Jesus I find new inspiration: as wise men sought out the holy babe, so does wisdom seek out the Christ in me, the glory that was with me before the world was made. Pure light in me is illumined by the spirit of life, and I am born into a spiritual understanding of God as man. With this birth, I embody the very love of God, and goodwill to men. And so it is.   AMEN

• TRINITY CANDLES

*T*he Christ candle is already lit, because it never goes out. Before Abraham was, it is. The trinity candles will now be lighted, because they represent aspects of the God-Being which involve the creative process, and so have relative being;

the blue candle (light it here) represents the father, the source, the creative principle, mind, the generative force or intelligence. The yellow candle (light it here) represents the soul, the Law, spirit, the formative principle. The green candle (light it here) represents the son, the effect, the body, the manifest world of forms, the thing that happens.

• CONGREGATIONAL CANDLE LIGHTING

*T*his is the act that makes the service. Your people will remember it from year to year. Along with the Good Friday Service, this is an outstanding spiritual event of the year.

The mechanics of this congregational lighting of candles must be worked out smoothly. In the simple form of the service, when the time comes the minister will make some appropriate remarks concerning the fact that "each individual must for himself ignite the light of his faith and his vision, and in symbolical commemoration of this spiritual awakening that comes with our experience here this evening, let each one of you now come forward, take up a candle from the table, and light it at the Christ candle. Then place it with a silent prayer of givingness into the bed of salt."

Some ministers have on hand "blessing cards" or scriptural passages typed out on slips of paper, and the people are invited to take one as they take the candle.

Having lighted their own candle, they return to their place and meditate on the particular passage on the slip or card which they took, or received, perhaps from a student standing with the minister at the candle table.

In a church which has a Prayer Chapel separate from the auditorium, a very wonderful variation is to have another Christ candle burning there, and have the congregation form a "Pilgrimage" column to the chapel, there to ignite their individual candles, carrying them lit back to the main auditorium to be placed in the bed of salt. Here, the minister makes the appropriate remarks about the inner significance through the ages of the "pilgrimage" idea. Present this symbology in a way to carry a spiritual meaning.

- **Lecture Notes**

(In the more elaborate service, there will be no time for a lecture. However, in the simple form, where a part of the hour or hour and a half remains, the leader can be prepared to give a brief concluding lesson on Christmas.)

*A*n outstanding characteristic of the churches of GOD UNLIMITED is emphasis on Law and each helping himself. We prove to our students that they can do the things we talk about. So we teach "treatment" and let the student learn to prove his dominion in life.

This is very good. But we then must bring the student further, into a more absolute realm, sharing with him that treatment becomes absolute to the degree that it ceases to be relative. This is from our University of Healing textbook from the course THE ART AND SCIENCE OF WHOLENESS. It is to remind us of the other pillar of love, balancing the pillar of Law. It is the presence contrasted to the principle.

The mystic Christ is the only begotten and eternal son of the only and one father-mother God We are here moving into a higher understanding of our teaching—moving from the science, through the philosophy, and into the real religion. The Christ shows us the way. It lives within us. We must, however, awaken to It. Paul said, "Awake thou that sleepest, and arise from the dead, and Christ shall give thee light."[3]

In the evening candlelight ceremony, we outwardly symbolized an inward and invisible grace, an awakening, a rebirth in the Christ spirit and the spirit of truth. We see that we partake of the nature of God, but that each consciously choose to take the goodness and the spirit of life. Each see the shining of his own candle of faith and strength and love. Light it from the one eternal Christ light of the world, that came into the world. It is the word, and the word was and is with God, and God is the word. In it is life, and that life is the light of man.

∞

---

3   Ephesians 5:14 [KJV]

Perfect
Love
Never
Goes
Out
Of
Style.

Be still,
And know
That I
Am God.

Psalm 46:10 [KJV]

Theme 9

ON
BEING
IMMORTAL

ON BEING IMMORTAL

*N*o matter who we are death not only seems final, it is final. The physical body is laid down as no longer useful. The viable form in which one lived is no longer going to be present.

We allay our fears saying the life the person lived is his memorial, his monument. However, this does little good to those "left" behind to live without this person who was very special to their beloved ones. Death is cruel to the living because they are not also dead. If the living were "dead" the living would no longer wish that loved one return to life or live forever in their human form.

What is death but laying down the illusion of a physical form to return to "awareness" of immortality. If we all believed this and our lives were the least bit difficult here, we would commit suicide at the least little abrasion life threw at us. Perhaps we live because we do not know our immortality.

We live because we have chosen this adventure with all its ups and downs to see how quickly we can remember our purpose and to live the purpose of being divine. Hence, to commit suicide delays our ultimate journey.

Science tells us there is neither time nor space. Eternity is now. Actually we are living on an infinite number of dimensions now. We live on Earth and other places equal to Earth and other places more mystically different from Earth.

Our essence is not our illusion in its multiplicity and diversity. Our essence is our oneness expressing as uniquenesses in a neverending progression.

Since we are humans we think in the framework of being wanted, needed, loved, sharing, experiencing. However, we do the same thing at the movies. When we see a film we become one with it and forget our otherness. We can see many films in a short time. In much the same way we live many lifetimes at once.

Our life right now is but one dimension. It is not final as it may seem.

For instance:

*P*hysical death always seems so final to ob-
servers. This is true in the laboratory of Earth or
the cosmic "Big Bang." Why does this seem so
total and lacking in continuity—it seems this way
because this transition is seen as a finality rather
than a continuum of "life" and "existence" and
"reality."

Life is the active expression of archetypal concepts. Consistent with "Thoughts are things." We
can recognize ideas are eternal. We know concepts
in their archetypal expression never change.
Change comes about through illusions. The pure
integral aspect of a concept remains forever the
same. Only as it is enhanced by imagination and
illusion does its variable nature demonstrate.
Also, the variable nature is unstable and disap-
pears. The archetypal purity never changes—but
this concept is also never SEEN.

So as we mourn the passing of illusions, we
have many phantasms whose insubstantial image
is but a chimera—never was real, but since we
think we see them we call them concrete.

All experiences—animal-mineral-vegetable—
assume make-believe costumes expressing dy-
namic expressions of firmness. The diversity is
limitless. Only the archetypal reality stands immortal.

As a minister we know the truth about life and
illusions. From our stability we show empathy to
our parishioners and to ourselves.   ∞

To every thing
There is a season,
And a time to every purpose
Under heaven:

A time to be born,
And a time to die;
A time to weep
and a time to laugh,
A time to mourn,
and a time to dance;

A time to get,
And a time to lose;
A time to keep,
And a time to pass away.

Ecclesiastes 3: 1,w,e,6

FUNERALS

*T*he service should not exceed twenty-five minutes. The organ plays fifteen minutes before the service, during the time friends and family are being seated. The mortician will seat the minister before the organist stops playing. The organist will need to know the last word of the service as a signal to begin playing the closing music.

The seating of the minister at the close of the service is a signal for the mortician to come forward. As the public begins to pass before the bier, the minister should stand quietly at one side. (See "Conduct of Ministers.")

Suggested Specific Order of Service

I
Opening statement

Scripture

Prayer

Scripture

Prayer

Scripture

Silent Meditation

Music

Obituary

Sermon

Prayer

Closing statement
(if interment at graveside.)

(Otherwise, brief committal
statements at end of service in chapel)

Twenty Third Psalm

Committal statements

Prayer

Closing Statement

II

Opening Statement

Scripture reading

Prayer

Music
(and/or solo)

Talk
(including short message for family)

Committal statement
(only if service is completed in chapel)

Short prayer

Music
(if two solos arranged)

Mortician officiates at viewing

III

Short opening prayer

Scripture reading

Opening Statement

Music

Talk

Twenty Third Psalm

Committal
(if completed at chapel)

Short prayer

Music

Mortician officiates at viewing

IV

Where lodge or patriotic ritual is included, adapt these to include whatever is necessary, perhaps omitting some steps.

Notes on Funeral Arrangements

When the undertaker calls and asks if you can take such and such a service, and your answer is "Yes," ask these six things:

1. Where and when is the service?

2. Who is the first next of kin, and do they want you to call. ("Do you think Mrs would appreciate a call from me?" If a member of your own group, naturally you will call without asking the undertaker.)

3. Do not ask about a fee or honorarium. However if you are called way out of your own district it is not only proper but advisable to ask the undertaker, in a pleasant way, whether arrangements will be made to take care of your travel expenses.

4. Is there to be music at the service—what type? Tell him that if so you will give the singer or musician the cue to fit in with your service when you arrive at the mortuary. (Always get there fifteen minutes early, for this purpose.)

5. Is the service complete at the chapel, or will there be a graveside committal? Where?

6. Tell the undertaker you will want to be provided, when you arrive at the chapel, with the customary "Officiant's Record" on the deceased— for your use for the obituary. THIS OFFICIANT'S RECORD MUST BE KEPT PERMANENTLY IN YOUR OFFICIAL CHURCH FILES.

MINISTER'S CONDUCT

*N*aturally the minister will dress appropriately.

In a town where the weather gets very hot and light suits are customary, and you know the family, you can ask the widow (or whoever it is) if the men plan to wear light or dark suits. If they wear light suits, you may do the same. Women ministers will follow the same rule.

The director will usher you to the rostrum at the right time. Be seated for a moment—usually as the music comes to a close. Then rise and begin the service. After the service sit for a moment to indicate the service is over. Then as the public begins coming forward to pass the bier you may stand quietly to one side. When the public is gone and the family comes forth to view the body you should step a few yards back into the chapel unless they wish to speak with you or you with them.

Where the service is complete at the chapel and when the family has departed in their car the minister is free to depart. Where there is an interment, the minister remains with the casket, walks before it as it is taken to be placed by the pallbearers in the coach and stands aside as it is placed in the coach. He generally rides in the coach with the body, although in special cases where it seems advisable he may drive his own car in the procession.

At the cemetery the minister alights from the coach or approaches it at once from his own car and stands aside as preparations are made to place the casket on the cart provided. When the director indicates the minister will lead the procession to the grave he stands aside while the casket is placed and then at a nod from the director, takes his place at the head of the casket, (always see that you know which is the head of the casket at the grave) and begins the committal service.

When the minister has finished he should step back or aside a few feet to indicate the service is completed. He should remain until the family has withdrawn unless they show signs of an unusually prolonged family reunion, with conversation (it happens), in which case the minister can step up to the next of kin and ask to be excused.

BURIAL RHETORIC

*T*he minister may read one of the following statements to begin the service:

We have come together this day to consider the continuity of life—in this instance the continuity of the life of our beloved friend.

He that dwelleth in the secret place of the most High shall abide under the shadow of the Almighty.[1] His place is found in peace. Let us now enter into that place. (This is used literally as the first thing the minister says, while seated when

---

1   Psalms 91:1 [KJV]

first ushered to his place, and as the music comes to a close. Then he rises and goes on with the service.)

The closing statement that goes with this particular "Order of Service"—No. **III** above, is as follows:

Bless the lord, o my soul: and all that is within me, bless his holy name.$_2$ The God in me salutes the God in you. And we go forth in peace.

Poems:

When Earth 's Last Picture Is Painted, Rudyard Kipling

The Rose Beyond the Wall

The Traveler, James Dillet Freeman

In My Father's House, Robert Freeman

Immortality from *The Song Celestial*, Holmes

Snowbound, John Greenleaf Whittier

Waiting, John Burroughs

Thanatopsis, Bryant

Note: Many funeral parlors put out a little booklet for families which contain various poems; ministers might check with the local funeral directors.

Silent meditation as part of the service:

---

2   Psalms 103:1 [KJV]

After the prayer and scripture, the minister may say:

Friends, in the belief of our church we grant a very special place to silent meditation where one finds that in the silence the spirit of God that dwells within everyman will speak in an inner realization. Let us now quietly realize together that everpresent love of God which is the Law of eternal life.

(Here can be added the words of Longfellow:)

Let us then labor for an inward stillness
An inward stillness and an inward healing:
That perfect silence where the lips and heart
Are still, and we no longer entertain
Thoughts that man has thought, vain opinions.
But God alone speaks in us, and we wait
In singleness of heart, that we may know
His Will, and in the silence of our spirits
That we do His Will, and do that only.
For God's Will for each of us is that we
Live and be happy and truly enjoy our lives.[3]

The minister stands in silence for a moment. Then music may follow. Following this the minister rises to give the obituary remarks and the sermon, etc.

---

3   Longfellow

Selected Scripture Passages

- Whither shall I go from thy Spirit? or whither shall I flee from thy presence? If I ascend up into heaven, thou art there: . . . If I take the wings of the morning, and dwell in the uttermost parts of the sea: even there shall thy hand lead me, and thy right hand shall hold me. If I say, surely the darkness shall cover me: even the night shall be light about me. Yea, the darkness hideth not from thee: but the night shineth as the day: the darkness and the light are both alike to thee.[4]

- Let not your heart be troubled: ye believe in God, believe also in me. In my Father's house are many mansions: if it were not so, I would have told you. I go to prepare a place for you. Peace I leave with you, my peace I give unto you. Let not your heart be troubled, neither let it be afraid.[5]

- The last enemy that shall be destroyed is death . . . . There is natural body, and there is spiritual body . . . the second man is the Lord from heaven . . . . There are also celestial bodies, and bodies terrestrial: but the glory of the celestial is one, and the glory of the terrestrial is another. There is one glory of the sun, another glory of the moon, and another glory of the stars: for one star differeth from another star in glory.[6]

---

[4]   Psalm 139:7-12
[5]   John 14:1-3; 27
[6]   I Corinthians 15:26, 44,47,40,41

TWENTY-THIRD PSALM (KJV)

The Lord is my shepherd; I shall not want. He maketh me to lie down in green pastures: he leadeth me beside the still waters.

He restoreth my soul: he leadeth me in the paths of righteousness for his name's sake.

Yea, though I walk through the valley of the shadow of death, I will fear no evil: for thou art with me; thy rod and thy staff they comfort me.

Thou preparest a table before me in the presence of mine enemies: thou anointest my head with oil; my cup runneth over.

Surely goodness and mercy shall follow me all the days of my life: and I will dwell in the house of the LORD *forever.*

(**Note:** See further scriptural suggestions under Jewish funeral services.)

SOLOS

In My House of Mansions, James MacDonald

The Lord's Prayer, Malotte

The Beatitudes, Malotte

Great Peace Have They, James Rogers

OBITUARY STATEMENTS

*S*uggested service form for Obituary Statement:

Friends, our service today marks the transition from one plane of life to another of (person's first name) who came into this world (date) at (place and state) and passed into the next plane of life on (date of death) at (time).

Whatever personal remarks, if any are to be made, are appropriately made at this point, preceding the sermon and leading into it.

Generally speaking, and certainly where the minister is not personally acquainted with either the deceased or the family calling upon his services, the bare obituary is sufficient. The day of eulogies is passed, except in the case of public figures or in the case of personal friends. The prolonged obituary or eulogy is not appropriate in the case of impersonal calls upon the minister for his funeral service.

On the other hand, it is never correct to omit the reference to the person for whom these services are being done, as some ministers have done.

There might well be added to the notes above that following the formal obituary statement, the following can be added:

(Person's name) leaves with us the following immediate family members: (his/her) (wife/husband) (names), brother (names), sister (names), sons (names), daughters (names) and others (names of close personal family or devoted friends and associates of a very personal relationship) (give the name in each instance).

Here may follow the Sermon remarks.

SUGGESTIONS REGARDING JEWISH SERVICE

*T*he minister should take his scriptural reading from the "Old Testament" and base his talk on the Mosaic Truth Teaching. God should not be addressed as: "The Deity" nor as "Our Father." **"O Lord" or "O God" are acceptable.**

Suggested scriptures:

Whither shall I go from thy spirit? or whither shall I flee from thy presence? If I ascend up into heaven, thou art here: If I make my bed in hell, behold, thou art there. If I take the wings of the morning, and dwell in the uttermost parts of the sea; Even there shall thy hand lead me, and thy right hand shall hold me. If I say, Surely the dark-

ness shall cover me, even the night shall be light about me. Yea, the darkness hideth not from thee; but the night shineth as the day: the darkness and the light are both alike to thee. [7]

Because he has set his love upon me, therefore I will deliver him; I will set him on high, because he has known my name. He shall call upon me, and I will answer him; I will be with him in trouble; I will deliver him and honor him. With long life I will satisfy him, and shew him my salvation. [8]

All the commandments which I command thee this day shall ye observe to do, that ye may live, and multiply, and go in and possess the land which the Lord sware unto your fathers. And thou shalt remember all the way which the Lord thy God led thee these forty years in the wilderness, to humble thee, and to prove thee, to know what was in thine heart, whether thou wouldst keep his commandments, or no. And he humbled thee, and suffered thee to hunger, and fed thee with manna, which thou knewest not, neither did thy fathers know; that he might make thee know that man doth not live by bread only, but by every word that proceedeth out of the mouth of the Lord doth man live. [9]

Hear, O Israel: The Lord our God is one Lord. [10]

---

7   Psalms 139:7-12
8   Psalms 91:14-16
9   Deuteronomy 8:1-3
10   Deuteronomy 6:4

LODGE PARTICIPATION

*G*enerally speaking the regular service should be short and be five to ten minutes. It is advisable to ask the funeral director concerning the time needed by the lodge. The lodge ceremony generally follows the regular service. If it can be lovingly arranged, it is well to have the lodge ceremony first inasmuch as their message often leaves a feeling of heaviness which we can counteract.

PATRIOTIC CEREMONY

*W*here the United States Government provides a flag on a veteran's casket, it may be taken up, folded and presented by the mortician to the minister for presentation to the next of kin.

If a veteran's organization participated in the service, however, their leader properly makes the presentation. The flag is presented to the next of kin, "in the name of the President of the United States of America, in grateful appreciation of the service rendered by (veteran's name)."

This flag presentation is usually taken care of after the public has viewed the remains and departed, and after the family has finished their own last viewing and have been seated for a few moments.

COMMITTAL SERVICE I

*C*herishing memories that are forever sacred, sustained by a faith that is stronger than death, comforted by the knowledge of life that is endless, we commit this mortal body to its final resting place, the elements from which it came; and realize that in so doing we are honoring the memory of this dear one who has gone before. We realize that the spirit of our beloved friend goes into more glorious experiences and shall continue on its forward, ever upward spiral, a journey into a more beautiful expression of eternity.

A short prayer.

COMMITTAL SERVICE II

*R*ead the Twenty-Third Psalm.

Man's earthly body is a sacred temple in which he dwells, and when he leaves it for a new experience in a higher life, it is fitting that the former temple be honored, and so we do now commit with love this body unto the elements from which it came, knowing that the spirit is no longer here. God's natural beauty is all about, and our thoughts will be of the living spirit triumphant, now free, and ever unfolding wherever unfolding. And we shall meet again.

Prayer invoking guidance, blessing and release. Know "Thy Will is done."

Closing statement.

GRAVESIDE SERVICE

*S*ometimes the minister will be asked to give a committal only, or a "graveside" service. This may be where a minister in another town has taken the chapel service, but calls on the minister in the location of the cemetery to take the committal, or it may be a case where the family is small, or there is only some friend, and no public service is desired, but a clergyman is wanted for the actual burial.

Each of these points should be made brief, in the case of this type of service; yet, where only this service is given the deceased, it is well to include all these points as they will not have been given at a chapel service.

1. Opening Statement

2. Scripture

3. Prayer—blessing occasion

4. Silent meditation

5. *Twenty-Third Psalm*

6. Very brief remarks, along sermon lines

7. Committal statements (as elsewhere)

If a flag is used by a lodge, its removal and holding is taken care of by the lodge.   ∞

MEMORIAL SERVICE

A considerable number of families seek to simplify the funeral service. They do not wish a formal funeral service but prefer a memorial service to be conducted in a chapel or a church sometime after the passing of the deceased. The suggested orders of service above can be used as a guide in the conduct of the service.

The following service brings in the use of a wide variety of metaphysical concepts and a very positive approach to death.

It is a memorial service which has all of the elements of totally uplifting the consciousness of the relatives and friends of the deceased.

Opening Prayer

*W*e are here for a joyful occasion, (person's name) has graduated to a higher expression of life. How magnificent that in the span (he/she) has lived, (he/she) was able to complete (his/her) growth on this plane. In that love, that joy, that harmony, we see (person's first name) rising into that greater experience of life that lies before (him/her) now in (his/her) oneness with God. We revel with (him/her) in this great achievement in joy and harmony, and we say thank you God for letting (him/her) join the wonderful infinite presence in totality once again.

And so it is!

Jesus said:

Let not your hearts be troubled; believe in God, believe also in me. In my Father's house are many rooms, if it were not so, would I have told you that I go to prepare a place for you? And when I go and prepare a place for you, I will come again and will take you to myself, that where I am you may be also. [11]

The Lord is my shepherd; I shall not want.

He maketh me to lie down in green pastures: he leadeth me beside the still waters.

---

[11]   John 15:1-3 [Lamsa]

He restoreth my soul: he leadeth me in the paths of righteousness for his name's sake.

Yea, though I walk through the valley of the shadow of death, I will fear no evil for thou art with me; thy rod and thy staff they comfort me.

Thou preparest a table before me in the presence of mine enemies; thou anointest my head with oil: my cup runneth over.

Surely goodness and mercy shall follow me all the days of my life: and I will dwell in the house of the Lord forever. [12]

---

12   Twenty-Third Psalm

The following may be used for children:

*P*arents are but the receptacle
Through which new beings have chosen
Admittance into this world.
They come to fulfill
Their own scheduled plans.

Leave them the freedom of choice
For in them lies the future
Which only they can envision.
Love them, care for their physical self
But leave them margin to grow
In thought and being.

In them lies the new world
Only they can form and build.
Life is a continual change forward
Be not tempted to mold them to your pattern
Be joyful in the new they bring with them
Love them for what they are
Knowing greatness lies ahead.

Only God within them can direct their course
Always aware of the wishes of the infinite
Stand aside and let live and give way
To the new growth and concepts
Even as divine love is pleased
With the directness of your children,
It is no less pleased
With the balanced gladness
With which you give way to the new.

The following may be used for adults:

You ask about death:
Look unto the living for your answer
Is not life and death
But the two sides of the same coin?
He who is blind knows not
The contrast of day and night
Neither does he who has not lived well.

As the Earth conceals the life of seeds
So does imagination hold
Cupped in its hands all reality
Awaiting the opening
Of your heart and mind
Eternity itself will speak to you
Fear neither side of the coin.

For death but brings you face to face
With the King of Kings
And you stand in awe
As the wind swiftly flutters
Around your head
And you bask in the rays
Of the sunlight.

As God speaks:
"Well done, my Son!"
As you reach the summit
Surrounded by radiating rays of light
Your silence is transformed
Into a glorious choral of song
And you dance in ecstasy of a new life!

LET US TURN WITHIN ONCE AGAIN AND RECOG-
NIZE THAT (person's first name), INDEED IS—

*B*orn *of Eternal Day*

*Child of all good, you are born of Eternal Day.
There is no evening of the Soul, for it lives forever.
It is deathless and perfect, complete and one with
the Everlasting.*

*No thought of tomorrow can disturb the calm of
him who knows that Life is one Eternal Day.*

*No fear can enter when Love reigns, and Rea-
son keeps faith with Hope.*

*The thoughts of the tomorrows and the yester-
days are swallowed up in the great realization of
the Perfect Here and the Complete Now.*[13]

*T*his is the truth that we all know and accept,
this is the experience of God living moving and
breathing in and through our lives.   AMEN

We are born out of the heart of God to express
himself. From him we came and to his loving
presence we go during each pause on our upward
spiral to perfection.

We are immortal! We are spiritual beings expressing for a time, using the physical vehicles we

---

13   Ernest Holmes

call our bodies until we no longer need them in our journey of growing in conscious oneness with our creator. When death comes this I AM appears to be no longer.

Our being chose a physical body here so it evolved one, but when by reason of accident, illness or old age, the physical body is no longer an adequate instrument through which our being may function, it lays the present body aside and continues to function in a more subtle one.

(Here give some words about the members of the family and how the deceased responded to them and their relationship if you know it.)

It was surely hard for (him/her) to choose to make (his/her) step into eternity and leave this experience of living.

That was the kind of person (he/she) was and is, and (he/she) moved on to a higher expression of life we know very little about.

Could money have brought this inheritance that (person's name) has given to the world, to those in (his/her) family, to those (his/her) life have touched—these are but a few of the eternal qualities of charisma that (person's name) takes with (him/her) on (his/her) upward spiral. So we prepare not to die, but to live—the thought of death should slip from our consciousness altogether and when this great event of our being takes place, it should be beautiful, it should be sublime, a glorious experience, as the eagle freed from its cage, soars to its native heights, so our being, freed from the home of heavy flesh rises to the father's house, naked and unafraid.

We can think of (person's name) in (his/her) experience of settling down to sleep in the evening like unto Jonathan Livingston Seagull when the white gulls came to guide him on higher:

They came in the evening, then, and found Jonathan gliding peaceful and alone through his beloved sky. The two gulls that appeared at his wings were pure as starlight, and the glow from them was gentle and friendly in the high night air. But most lovely of all was the skill with which they flew, their wingtips moving a precise and constant inch from his own.

Without a word, Jonathan put them to his test, a test that no gull had ever passed. He twisted his wings, slowed to a single mile per hour above stall. The two radiant birds slowed with him, smoothly, locked in position. They knew about slow flying.

He folded his wings, rolled, and dropped into a dive to a hundred ninety miles per hour. They dropped with him, streaking down in flawless formation.

At last he turned that speed straight up into a long vertical slowroll. They rolled with him, smiling.

He recovered to level flight and was quiet for a time before he spoke: "Very well, " he said, "who are you?"

"We're from your Flock, Jonathan. We are your brothers." The words were strong and calm. "We've come to take you higher, to take you home."

"Home, I have none. Flock, I have none. I am an Outcast. And we fly now at the peak of the Great Mountain Wind. Beyond a few hundred feet, I CAN LIFT THIS OLD BODY NO HIGHER."

"But you can, Jonathan. For you have learned. One school is finished, and the time has come for another to begin."

As it has shined across him all his life, so understanding lighted that moment for Jonathan Seagull. They were right. He COULD FLY higher, and it was time to go home.

He gave one last long look across the sky, across that magnificent silver land where he had learned so much.

"I'm ready," he said at last.

And Jonathan Livingston Seagull rose with the two starbright gulls to disappear into a perfect dark sky.[14]

I shall never die, for the spirit within me is God and cannot change.

My life is hid within the universe of love and light, and that light shall live forever.

Go, fear of death and change; begone from my thought, fear of death and uncertainty. That which is cannot become that which is not; and that which I am can never change. The spirit of eternity is

---

14   Richard Bach

enthroned within me and the life of endless ages flows through my being. From eternity to eternity my life flows along its way of peace and harmony. Time brings but more glory to crown me with its pleasures. My life is forever.

*E*very life that is lived gives us the privilege of growing by its very existence. Let's consider the life of (person's name) as a challenge to us, (he/she) was a normal person, one who cried when (he/she) was hurt, one who knew what (he/she) wanted to do and proceeded to do it at every point.

But of all things (he/she) is a perfect idea in the mind of God. (He/she) loves each of us even now as (he/she) moves into this greater experience of life. How will we live our lives from this day forward, will the monument (he/she) gave to us, a monument of a loving life, guide us to be more beautiful, more complete persons, who will be more loving to every person we experience, or will we mourn (his/her) passing and be sorry for ourselves not to have the joy of (his/her) companionship.

The challenge, the joy and the experience is ous, let us each one consider what (person's name) has said to us with (his/her) life:

"*I live fully and beautifully and well, don't mourn for me, but take the gift I have given you of my love, however large or small that token may have been, and run with it with enthusiasm and joy and the expectation that these are the joyful experiences of life, for this is what God created us to do, to run with enthusiasm and joy, the privilege of the life that we lead.*"

*O*ur father, what a privilege it is to share our lives in this world of companionship and joy, what a privilege it is to make each life we touch a more joyous and more beautiful experience. We take this heritage that (person's name) has given us and of (his/her) love and we embellish the world in which we live, by adding that little bit of love we have to share with others and we say thank you father for this wonderful privilege, this wonderful gift, this wonderful life of (person's name in full) given to us so lovingly from thee.

So it is and so it shall ever be!

Prayer

Let us turn within for a moment and recognize that we are chosen children of the most high, and:

When death shall come
And the spirit, freed,
shall mount the air,
And wander afar
in that great no-where,
It shall go as it came,
Freed from sorrow,
sin and shame;
And naked and bare,
through the upper air
Shall go alone to that
great no-where.
Hinder not its onward way,
Grieve not o're its form of clay,
For the spirit,
freed now from clod,
Shall go alone to meet its God.

Ernest Holmes

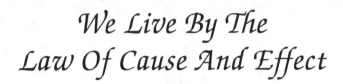

We Live By The Law Of Cause And Effect

and other RULES

Theme 10

LEGAL

God
Is not only true
But truth itself.

Pope Leo XIII

CERTIFICATES—DIPLOMAS
ORDINATION—DEGREES

*C*opies of the actual recognitions given to students who successfully complete the programs of the University of Healing are reproduced here.

These nonacademic certificates are awarded to candidates who achieve a high level of excellence in both scholastic studies, religious contemplations and spiritual integrity through the six major programs of the University of Healing: Ordination, Practitioner, Bachelor of Philosophy. Master of Healing Science, Doctor of Philosophy and Doctor of Divinity.

The University of Healing undergraduate college degree of BACHELOR OF PHILOSOPHY is earned for the achievement of a high scholastic and educational level in the field of philosophy and religion through the studies of the undergraduate program of the University of Healing. Those students who have competently directed their diligent efforts to daily speaking their word, reading the word, and living by the indwelling divinity, over the period of the course work, have earned this nonacademic degree of competence in the eyes of the Board of Regents of the University of Healing.

The earned degree of PRACTITIONER is given to all those who complete the Practitioner Academy of the University. It is felt that those who have completed this study are well qualified in every way to act and serve as a practitioner for themselves and others. They have the underlying truths which aid them in establishing their relationship to the friend and themselves.

The certificate of ORDINATION is given to all of those candidates who successfully complete the Ministerial Academy of study at the University. For they now are able to serve competently as ministers of truth and may go out into all the world showing themselves as living examples of what they have learned and more, WHAT THEY PERSONALLY BELIEVE!

The degree of MASTER OF HEALING SCIENCES is earned by those who have fulfilled their undergraduate work and have gone on to show themselves capable in the masterful art of healing consciousness. Graduate School takes determined dedication on the part of the student and through applied sincerity and dedicated understanding, the candidates achieve excellence in this scientific art.

The Post Graduate Professional Division degree of DOCTOR OF PHILOSOPHY is earned by those who are unlimited in their consciousness and have sought to attain the very highest possible mastership of the ART AND SCIENCE OF WHOLENESS. And having done so, writing a dissertation on healing that reveals their understanding of the truth about themselves and the world about them which THEY have CREATED. These candidates are those who know no bounds but soar into spiritual awareness and total wholeness in every aspect of their beingness.

The Post Graduate Professional Division ABSOLUTE Seminary degree of DOCTOR OF DIVINITY is earned through study and recognition that all begins and ends in each being, as taught by Jesus, Buddha, Mohammed, the Bible, and religious philosophies universewide. This degree shows the world how spiritually dedicated the holder stands.

Here are the six certificates earned by to those candidates who have successfully completed the courses of the University of Healing. All of the degrees are 8½ by 11 inches in size on parchment.

All awards are subject to approval by the Board of Regents of the University of Healing.

Also shown here is the TEACHING CHARTER and the CHURCH CHARTER.

University of Healing

a church of
meditation, teaching and healing

College of the
Art and Science of Wholeness

and by virtue of the authority in them vested
have conferred upon

Charles Brown

the degree of
Bachelor of Philosophy

with all the Honors,
Privileges and Obligations thereto pertaining.

Given at Campo, California
1 January 1997

Chairman of the Board of Regents

President of the University

University of Healing

The Regents of the University and The Practitioner Academy
on the recommendation
of the President's Council on Church Affairs of
God Unlimitd, a Church of Meditation,
Teadching and Healing
And by virtue of the authority in them vested have found
qualified and have conferred upon

Charles Brown

the degree of

Practitioner

with all the Honors,
Privileges and Obligations thereto pertaining.

Given at Campo, California
1 January 1997

Chairman of the Board of Regents   President of the University

God Unlimited

a church of
meditation, teaching and healing

Credentials and Certificate of Ordination

This is to certify that
The Ministerial Academy of
The Church of God Unlimited finds

Charles Brown

is worthy and well endowed spiritually and educationally to carry on the work of teaching the truth, healing, preaching the word, being an example of pure living, and to perform all the functions of the ministry, and by the powers vested in God Unlimited, is hereby ordained to said office.

Given at Campo, California
1 January 1997

GOD UNLIMITED
UNIVERSITY OF HEALING
1975

President of the Church

University of Healing

The Regents of the University on the
recommendation of the Faculty of the

Graduate
School

and by virtue of the authority in them vested
have conferred upon

Charles Brown

the degree of

Master of Healing Sciences

with all the Honors,
Privileges and Obligations thereto pertaining.

Given at Campo, California
1 January 1997

Chairman of the Board of Regents

President of the University

University of Healing

The Regents of the University on the
recommendation of the Faculty of the

Post Graduate
Professional Division

and by virtue of the authority in them vested
have conferred upon

Charles Brown

the degree of
Doctor of Philosophy

with all the Honors,
Privileges and Obligations thereto pertaining.

Given at Campo, California
1 January 1997

Chairman of the Board of Regents

President of the University

University of Healing

The Regents of the University on the
recommendation of the Faculty of the

Post Graduate Professional Division
Absolute Seminary

and by virtue of the authority in them vested
have conferred upon

Charles Brown

the degree of

Doctor of Divinity

with all the Honors,
Privileges and Obligations thereto pertaining.

Given at Campo, California
1 January 1997

Chairman of the Board of Regents   *President of the University*

Teaching Charter

This is to certify the
Church of God Unlimited

finds the

Temple Of Awareness

is a qualified teaching center of the
Church of God Unlimited

Upon completion of approved courses student
certificates may be awarded countersigned by
the Church of God Unlimited and the University
of Healing of Campo California.

1 January 1997

Shirley L. Perry

Chairman of the Board of Regents

signature

President of the University

Church Charter

This is to certify the
Church of God Unlimited

finds the

Temple Of Awareness

Has fulfilled all requirements and is affiliated
as a Member Church in good standing of the
Church of God Unlimited in Campo California.

This certificate is renewed annually

1 January 1997

Chairman of the Board   **President of the Church**

MEMBER CHURCH CONCEPT

*A*ll churches or groups which desire to affiliate with the tax exempt church of GOD UNLIMITED/UNIVERSITY OF HEALING must fill in an AFFILIATION AGREEMENT received from headquarters and then send it in to headquarters with their check for $100 to be considered for association with the parent organization. For further information write to the President, God Unlimited/University of Healing, 1101 Far Valley Road, Campo, California 91906-3213 and copies of the agreement in this manual and other materials will be forwarded to you.

Anyone who wants to become a church under the tax exemption determination letter of the parent group is required by law to become a nonprofit group or corporation in their respective state which can be done for a minimum cost, for the tax exemption status to be held valid by city, county, state and federal agencies, the member church must be under the direction and legal responsibilities of the parent organization. For this reason the *Articles of Incorporation* and *Bylaws* which have been approved by the governmental agencies involved.

For more details contact God Unlimited/University of Healing headquarters.

AGREEMENT OF AFFILIATION FOR MEMBER CHURCHES

*T*his agreement between God Unlimited/University of Healing, a California religious, educational and charitable nonprofit corporation hereinafter called the CHURCH and _____ a nonprofit group or corporation hereinafter called the MEMBER CHURCH, is made on the basis of the following recital of facts:

The CHURCH is the central organization of an international interdenominational religious, educational and charitable group comprised of the CHURCH and of various local groups, churches and international churches affiliated with it, established and existing for the purpose of worship and education on the basis of the principles expressed by the Church of God Unlimited and the University of Healing.

The MEMBER CHURCH is an organized and existing group or church which desires to become fully affiliated with the CHURCH and to take part in its church life and organization.

Therefore in consideration of the mutual covenants set forth in this **Agreement of Affiliation**, the CHURCH and the MEMBER CHURCH agree as follows:

Use of Name

The CHURCH grants to the MEMBER CHURCH the right to adopt and use a name including the words "God Unlimited." The member church understands and agrees that such name and all right, title and interest therein is the property of the CHURCH and agrees that it shall be entitled to the use of such name or terms only so long as it shall be and remain a church fully affiliated and in good standing with the CHURCH, and if and when such good standing or affiliation shall no longer be in effect all such use shall be terminated forthwith.

Maintenance of Member Church

The MEMBER CHURCH agrees to maintain and operate a group or CHURCH OF GOD UNLIMITED in full affiliation and good standing with the CHURCH, for the purpose of worship, teaching, demonstrating and education within the principles as expressed in the University of Healing and as taught by the CHURCH, and agrees that its assets and properties are and shall be reserved and dedicated for church purposes. In connection therewith, the MEMBER CHURCH further agrees and understands as follows:

- The MEMBER CHURCH, its Board of Directors, members and officers shall be subject to the ecclesiastical law and authority of the CHURCH, which shall control in all matters of ecclesiastical jurisdiction.

- The MEMBER CHURCH will hire and retain as minister only those persons who shall have been duly ordained and accredited, and who shall be and remain in good standing as ministers of the CHURCH and will endorse and support the work of only those Practitioners, Counselors and Ministers of GOD UNLIMITED who shall have been duly licensed as such by the CHURCH.

- The MEMBER CHURCH shall not support, encourage, promote or endorse the practice or use of an other philosophy, practice or ceremony not within the principles of GOD UNLIMITED, provided that the foregoing shall not be construed to prohibit educational discussion which may relate to such matters.

- The MEMBER CHURCH agrees that its affiliation with the CHURCH may be terminated by it only as provided in its bylaws on file with the CHURCH at its headquarters.

- The MEMBER CHURCH shall establish clear and effective standards for the admission of members and shall maintain its membership books and records in an orderly and businesslike manner so that the number of members, and names and addresses, shall at all times be readily ascertainable to any person having a proper interest therein. Such membership records shall at all times be available to the CHURCH.

Minister of Member Church

The MEMBER CHURCH agrees that the office of Minister thereof shall automatically become vacant if and when official recognition of any Minister shall be suspended or revoked by the Church Council of the CHURCH, and further agrees as follows:

The Minister shall have and exercise all the powers of, duties and prerogatives usually accorded to a clergyman including, without limitation, the planning, teaching and supervision of all classes of instruction, both accredited and nonaccredited; and the leadership, supervision and conduct of the activities of all organizations and groups within the MEMBER CHURCH, and of religious, educational, counseling, fellowship and worship activities of the MEMBER CHURCH.

When the office of Minister becomes vacant, the Board of Directors of the MEMBER CHURCH shall appoint a Ministerial Procurement Committee. The committee shall proceed to contact the Administrator of the Department of Member Churches of the CHURCH, and through him and the

Church Council of the CHURCH, shall meet with and consider qualified candidates to fill such vacancy. The Committee shall select one such candidate and present his name and qualifications to the Board of Directors. If the Board shall approve such selection, it shall extend a call to such person to become the Minister of the MEMBER CHURCH, and if it shall not so approve, the Committee shall present such further names as may be necessary to obtain a selection satisfactory to the Board of Directors. The terms of employment of such Minister shall be determined by the Board and shall be specified in any call which it may extend, and upon acceptance of such call by the Minister, an agreement of employment shall be deemed to be in effect between the MEMBER CHURCH and such Minister.

Status of Member Church

The CHURCH agrees that the MEMBER CHURCH shall have full standing, and all the rights and privileges, of an affiliated church, as set forth in the Bylaws and other instruments of the CHURCH relating to affiliated churches, as presently in effect and as hereafter adopted. The MEMBER CHURCH charter will be renewed annually.

Accredited Courses

The MEMBER CHURCH shall only be entitled to teach courses accredited by the University of Healing as prescribed by the Board of Regents of the CHURCH, and graduates thereof shall receive appropriate recognition certificates and diplomas issued by the church, provided, however, that prior to the teaching of any such courses the MEMBER

CHURCH shall have made appropriate application for a TEACHING CHARTER to said Board of Regents, which Charter shall have been granted and provided further that such teaching of course work shall continue only so long as said Charter shall remain in effect and in good standing. All inquiries or matters pertaining to this paragraph should be taken up with the University of Healing—Attention Director of Education.

Assets and Liabilities of the Parties

Each of the parties hereto understands and agrees that neither claims or has any right, title or interest in the assets or properties of the other, and that neither shall be or become responsible for the liabilities, or performance of any of the obligations presently existing or which may be incurred, by the other.

No Ordination, Licensing or Branches

The MEMBER CHURCH agrees that so long as this Agreement is in effect it will not ordain or license ministers or license practitioners or teachers, and will not establish any branch church, it being understood that all such matters are within the exclusive power and authority of the CHURCH. Except as defined in Article VIII, Section 3 of the approved Bylaws of the member church now on file at headquarters.

Apportionment Payments

As a MEMBER CHURCH we will provide to the CHURCH our annual financial statement and tithe to the CHURCH ten percent of our monthly income from all sources.

A fee of one hundred dollars shall accompany this Agreement.

Duly Authorized Agreement

The undersigned officers of the MEMBER CHURCH hereby represent and warrant by their execution and delivery of this Agreement, and that the execution and delivery hereof for and on behalf of the MEMBER CHURCH has been duly and properly authorized by the Board of Directors and by the members, and by any and all other bodies, groups, committees and officers of the MEMBER CHURCH, the approval and consent of which may be necessary in order to constitute this Agreement as the valid and binding agreement and covenant of the MEMBER CHURCH.

Condition Subsequent To
Action of Church Council

The MEMBER CHURCH understands and agrees that the execution and delivery hereof on behalf of the CHURCH is fully subject to the express conditions subsequent that such execution and delivery, and the acceptance of the MEMBER CHURCH into the organization of the CHURCH as a church affiliated with the CHURCH, hereafter shall be approved by the duly adopted resolution of the CHURCH Council of the CHURCH and that this Agreement shall not be valid or binding upon the CHURCH for any purpose whatever unless so adopted and so approved. The CHURCH agrees to present this Agreement to said Church Council for action at the first practicable opportunity, and shall advise the MEMBER CHURCH of all action taken with respect thereto.

This Petition for affiliation shall be presented to the Church Council at the first regular meeting after being received in the Administrator's office, and held for final action at the following regular Council meeting.

In Witness Whereof, the undersigned file this Agreement of Affiliation at Campo, California, by their duly authorized representatives.

Member Church

Name: _____

Address: _____

City: _____ State: _____ Zip: _____

Country: _____

By: _____
      Minister, MEMBER CHURCH

By: _____
      President, Board of Directors, MEMBER CHURCH

God Unlimited/University of Healing

a California religious,
educational, charitable
nonprofit corporation

By: _____
      Minister, MEMBER CHURCH

By: _____
      President, Board of Directors, MEMBER CHURCH

Date: _____

LEGAL STANDING

*T*he following forms may be filled in as acceptable incorporation papers for any church affiliating with God Unlimited/University of Healing. Then file the filled in incorporation articles and bylaws, signed and notarized, with the signature of the incorporating officer on the Articles and Bylaws. Enclose a check for $30 to the State of California Nonprofit Corporation. Corporation Filing and Services Division, 1500 Eleventh Street, Sacramento CA, 95814. (916) 657-5448. Also secure in California Form 3500 from the State of California Franchise Tax Board, Sacramento CA 95857 (916) 657-5448; fill it in and sign form and enclose check for $25 to them. Secure Package 1023 from the Internal Revenue

under Section 501 (c) (3) APPLICATION FOR REC-
OGNITION OF EXEMPTION and fill in the forms
therein attaching to it the DETERMINATION LET-
TER given to all ordained ministers of GOD UN-
LIMITED who are seeking to establish their own
church activity. God Unlimited Ministers are
given the material only upon completing the AF-
FILIATION AGREEMENT with God Unlimited.

CALIFORNIA SECRETARY OF STATE

CORPORATE FILING AND SERVICES DIVISION

California nonprofit, nonstock corporations, for religious, charitable, social, educational, recreational or similar purposes are organized under the Nonprofit Corporation Law as embodied in the California Corporations Code beginning at Section 5000.

The three primary types of nonprofit corporations, namely, religious, public benefit and mutual benefit.

A corporation organized to operate a church or to be otherwise structured for primarily religious purposes is a nonprofit RELIGIOUS corporation.

THE FEE FOR FILING ARTICLES OF INCORPORATION ON BEHALF OF A NONPROFIT, NONSTOCK CORPORATION IS $30.00.

Additionally, the $800.00 minimum annual franchise tax must be remitted with the Articles of Incorporation or the proposed corporation must apply for, and have issued, exemption from payment of tax from the Franchise Tax Board before the articles may be filed. If an Application for Exemption from payment of tax is to be made, then the completed application (Form 3500), together with all attachments called for in the application instructions and the $25.00 application processing fee must be submitted to the Secretary of State with the original articles, at least four copies of the articles and the $30.00 Secretary of State filing fee.

The Secretary of State will certify two copies of the filed Articles of Incorporation without charge, **provided that the copies are submitted to the Secretary of State along with the original to be filed.** Any additional copies, submitted with the original, will be certified upon request with prepayment of $8.00 per copy.

When forming a new corporation you may also wish to contact one or more of the following agencies for additional information.

The Franchise Tax Board—for information regarding exemption and/or Franchise tax requirements.

- The Board of Equalization—for information regarding **sales tax** and/or use tax liability.

- The city and/or county clerk and/or recorder where the principal place of business is located—for information regarding business licenses, fictitious business names (if doing business under a name other than the corporate name), and for specific requirements regarding zoning, building permits, etc. based on the activities of the corporation.

- Internal Revenue Service (IRS)—for information regarding federal employee identification number.

Corporate Filing and Services Division
1500 Eleventh Street
Sacramento CA 95814
(916) 657-5448

ARTICLES OF INCORPORATION
OF

I

The name of this corporation is:

_____

II

A. This corporation is a RELIGIOUS CORPORATION and is not organized for the private gain of any person. It is organized under the Nonprofit Religious Corporation Law primarily for religious purposes.

B. The specific purpose of this corporation is to operate a religious teaching and/or worship center.

III

The name and address in the State of:

this corporation's initial agent for service of process is:

Name _____

Street Address_____

City _____ State_____ Zip_____

IV

A. This corporation is organized and operated exclusively for religious purposes within the meaning of Section 501 (c)(3) of the Internal Revenue Code.

B. No substantial part of the activities of this corporation shall consist of carrying on propaganda, or otherwise attempting to influence legislation, and the corporation shall not participate or intervene in any political campaign (including the publishing or distribution of statements) on behalf of any candidate for public office.

C. This corporation is formed as an affiliate organization with God Unlimited/University of Healing, a California nonprofit religious corporation, Campo California, and comes under its Internal Revenue Code Section 501 (c)(3) Determination Letter for tax exempt organizations.

V

The property of this corporation is irrevocably dedicated to religious purposes and no part of the net income or assets of this corporation shall ever inure to the benefit of any director, officer or member thereof or to the benefit of any private person. Upon the dissolution or winding up of the corporation, its assets remaining after payment, or provision for payment, of all debts and liabilities of this corporation shall be distributed to a non-profit fund, foundation or corporation which is organized and operated exclusively for religious purposes and which has established its tax exempt status under Section 501 (c)(3) of the Internal Revenue Code.

Date: _____

I hereby declare that I am the person who executed the foregoing Articles of Incorporation, which execution is my act and deed.

_____

Signature of Incorporator

_____

Typed Name of Incorporator

BYLAWS
OF (group/corporation)

bylaws for the regulation thereof, except as otherwise provided by statute or its articles.

Article I

AFFILIATION AND ECCLESIASTICAL AUTHORITY

Section 1   **AFFILIATION.** This religious (group /corporation), the

hereinafter called AFFILIATE, with GOD UNLIM-ITED/UNIVERSITY OF HEALING, a California nonprofit religious, corporation with offices in Campo California, an international interdenominational non-denominational religious corporation—and exists for the purpose of worship, teaching and demonstrating the principles of the philosophy entreating each individual to unfold the Divinity within themselves to its greatest and highest potential, as taught by the University of Healing. This AFFILIATE acknowledges that it has been chartered by GOD UNLIMITED/UNIVERSITY OF HEALING as an affiliate for such purposes and that it has been created under its sponsorship and guidance.

Section 2   **ECCLESIASTICAL AUTHORITY.** This AFFILIATE, its Board of Directors, Members, and Officers shall be subject to ecclesiastical law and the authority of GOD UNLIM-

ITED/UNIVERSITY OF HEALING in all matters lawfully within ecclesiastical jurisdiction.

Section 3   **COMMUNICATIONS.** This AFFILIATE shall keep the president of GOD UN-LIMITED/UNIVERSITY OF HEALING generally informed as to its affairs. Annually informing the president of its membership, officers, previous year's operating budget relative to its monthly apportionment or tithe to the headquarters of GOD UNLIMITED/UNIVERSITY OF HEALING.

Article II

OFFICES

Section 1   **PRINCIPAL OFFICE.** The principal office for the transaction of business of this AFFILIATE is located in _____ the County of _____, the State of _____, at address: _____ , The Board of Directors may change said principal office from one location to another. Any such change shall be noted on the Bylaws by the Secretary, opposite this section, or this section may be amended to state the new location.

Article III

MEMBERS

Section 1   **ELECTION OF MEMBERS.** The Members of this AFFILIATE shall be those individual persons who are from time to time elected to membership by the Board of Directors.

Each Member shall agree to unfold his God nature to its highest and greatest potential.

Section 2   TERMINATION OF MEMBERSHIP. Membership in this AFFILIATE shall be terminated by death, resignation or withdrawal, or by resolution of the Board of Directors duly adopted.

Section 3   MEMBERSHIP RECORD. The Secretary of this religious AFFILIATE shall maintain an up-to-date permanent record containing the names and addresses of all Members of this AFFILIATE.

Article IV

MEETING OF MEMBERS

Section 1   PLACE OF MEETINGS. All meetings of Members shall be held either at the principal office or place of worship of this AFFILIATE or at any other place within or outside the state of incorporation which may be designated by the Board of Directors pursuant to authority herein granted the Board.

Section 2   ANNUAL MEETINGS. The annual meetings of Members shall be held on the second Sunday of each January. At such meetings reports of the affairs of the AFFILIATE shall be considered. Written notice of each annual meeting shall be given to each Member entitled. All such notices shall be sent to each Member entitled thereto not less than ten days nor more than thirty days before each annual meeting. Such notices shall specify the place, the day and hour of such meeting.

Section 3   SPECIAL MEETINGS. Subject to any applicable provision of law, the

Articles of Incorporation, or Bylaws, special meetings of the Members may be called at any time by the presiding officer of the Board of Directors or the Minister. Notice of any special meeting shall specify, in addition to the place, day and hour of such meetings, the general nature of the business to be transacted.

Article V

DIRECTORS

Section 1   POWERS. Subject to limitations of Articles of Incorporation, of the Bylaws, and of all applicable laws and subject to the duties of the Directors as prescribed by the Bylaws, all corporate power shall be exercised by or under the authority of, and the business and affairs of this AFFILIATE shall be controlled by, the Board of Directors. Without prejudice to such general powers, but subject to the same limitations, it is hereby expressly declared that the Directors shall have the following powers, to wit:

FIRST to conduct, manage and control the affairs and business of this AFFILIATE, and make such rules and regulations therefore not inconsistent with law, or with the Articles of Incorporation, with the Bylaws, as they may deem best;

SECOND to borrow money and incur indebtedness for the purpose of the AFFILIATE, and to cause to be executed and delivered therefore, in the corporate name, promissory notes, bonds, debentures, deeds, mortgages, pledges, hypothecations or the evidences of debt and securities therefore;

THIRD the President, at his discretion, to appoint an Executive Committee and other committees, and to delegate to the Executive Committee any of the powers or authority of the Board in management of the business and affairs of the AFFILIATE, except the power to adopt, amend or repeal the Articles or Bylaws.

Section 2 **NUMBER.** The authorized number of the Board of Directors may be the incorporator or more.

Section 3 **TERM OF OFFICE.** The Directors shall be elected to office annually.

Section 4 **PLACE OF MEETING**. The regular meetings of the Board of Directors shall be held at any place within or without the state of incorporation of this AFFILIATE which has been designated from time to time by resolution of the Board or by written consent of two-thirds of the members of the Board. In the absence of such designations regular meetings shall be held at the principal office of this AFFILIATE. Special meetings of the Board shall be held either at a place so designated or at the principal office.

Article VI

OFFICERS

Section 1 **OFFICERS.** The officers of this AFFILIATE shall be: President, Vice President, Secretary and Treasurer. This AFFILIATE may also have, at the discretion of the Board of

Directors, other officers. Any officer may hold more than one office.

Section 2   **RESIGNATION.** Any officer may resignate at any time by giving written or verbal notice to the Board of Directors, President, or Secretary.

Section 3   **PRESIDENT.** The President is the chief executive officer and has the general supervision of the spiritual life, business affairs, properties and employees. The President shall preside at all meetings of the Board of Directors, Membership and Executive Committee meetings, and define the duties of such committees; and shall have such other powers and perform such other duties as may be required from time to time.

Section 4   **VICE PRESIDENT.** The Vice President will conduct such duties as designated by the Board of Directors and/or the President. In the disability of the President, the Vice President shall have all powers and the responsibilities of the President, and shall perform all the duties of the President.

Section 5   **SECRETARY**. The Secretary shall keep or cause to be kept, at the principal office or such other place as the Board of Directors may order, the current certified By-laws; and a book of minutes of all meetings of the Directors and Members, with the time and place of holding, regular or special, and if special, how authorized, the notice thereof given, the names of those present at the Director's meeting, the number of persons present at Member's meetings, and the proceedings thereof. As above provided herein, the Secretary shall keep at the principal office the permanent membership record showing the names and addresses of the Members. The Secretary shall give, or cause to be given, notice of all meetings of the Members and of the Board of Directors required by the Bylaws or by law to be given, and shall have such other powers and perform such other duties as may be prescribed by the Board of Directors or the Bylaws.

Section 6   TREASURER. The treasurer shall keep and maintain, or cause to be kept and maintained, adequate and correct accounts of the properties and business transactions of this AFFILIATE, including accounts of its assets, liabilities, receipts, disbursements, gains, losses, capital and surplus. The books of account shall be open at all reasonable times to inspection by any Director or Member. The Treasurer shall be responsible for the preparation and distribution of annual financial statements. The Treasurer shall deposit all monies and other valuables in the name and to the credit of this AFFILIATE with such depositaries as may be ordered by the President whenever requested and give an account of all his transactions as Treasurer and of the financial condition of this AFFILIATE when requested and shall have such other powers and perform such other duties as may be prescribed by the Board of Directors or the Bylaws.

Article VII

MISCELLANEOUS

Section 1   CHECKS, DRAFTS, ETC. All checks, drafts, or other orders for payment of money, notes, or other evidences of indebtedness, issued in the name of or payable to this AFFILIATE shall be signed and endorsed by such person or persons and in such manner as, from time to time, shall be determined by a resolution of the Board.

Section 2 **CONTRACTS, ETC, HOW EXECUTED.** The Board of Directors, except as in the Bylaws otherwise provided, may authorize any officer or officers, agent or agents, to enter into any contract or execute any instrument in the name of and on behalf of this AFFILIATE, and such authority may be general or limited, to specific instances; and, unless so authorized by the Board of Directors, no Officer, agents or employees shall have any power or authority to make any agreement or create any obligation which shall bind this AFFILIATE or to pledge to the credit of this AFFILIATE or to render it liable for any purpose or in any amount. The Board of Directors hereby authorizes the President, to act in any and every fiduciary relationship on behalf of this AFFILIATE.

Section 3 **NO LIABILITIES.** Neither the Directors, Officers, nor Members of this AFFILIATE shall be personally liable for the debts, liabilities or obligations of this AFFILIATE.

Article VIII

RELIGIOUS
AFFILIATE MATTERS

NOTWITHSTANDING any other provision of the Bylaws, this AFFILIATE, its Board of Directors, Members and Officers are and at all times shall be subject to the following provisions:

Section 1 **MINISTER AND PRACTITIONERS.** This AFFILIATE will sustain as Minister, associate Ministers and Practitioners only those persons who shall have been duly credentialed, and who shall be and remain in good standing, as ministers of the CHURCH OF GOD UNLIMITED, and will endorse and support the work of only those practitioners of the CHURCH OF GOD UNLIMITED who shall have been duly licensed as such by the CHURCH OF GOD UNLIMITED.

Section 2   APPROVED PRACTICES. This AFFILIATE shall teach and practice the ideal "I am God, God I am" and all it means based on the UNI PRESS publication pamphlet entitled *Why I Can Say I Am God.* So long as this AFFILIATE is affiliated with GOD UNLIMITED/UNIVERSITY OF HEALING, this AFFILIATE will not ordain or license ministers, or license practitioners or teachers, and will not establish any branch AFFILIATE, and will be governed and abide by the rules, regulations and directives of GOD UNLIMITED/UNIVERSITY OF HEALING with respect to these matters.

Section 3   ORDAINING AND LICENSING. The minister of this AFFILIATE may submit their candidates for ordination, licensing and/or for practitioner and teacher status to GOD UNLIMITED/UNIVERSITY OF HEALING, and upon approval of their having passed the examinations and educational foundation requirements, they may, upon the recommendation of headquarters, then, on behalf of headquarters, thence ordain, license and/or qualify those so approved within the corporate structure of GOD UNLIMITED/UNIVERSITY OF HEALING.

Section 4   DISAFFILIATION. This AFFILIATE may terminate its affiliation with GOD UNLIMITED/UNIVERSITY OF HEALING of Campo California 91906-3213 U.S.A., only by a letter submitted and signed by the Board of Directors of this AFFILIATE stating its decision to disaffiliate. This clause may not be amended from this AFFILIATE's Bylaws so long as it is affiliated with GOD UNLIMITED/ UNIVERSITY OF HEALING.

Section 5   **NAME.** In case of disaffiliation by this AFFILIATE from GOD UNLIMITED/UNIVERSITY OF HEALING, this AFFILIATE shall promptly cease to use the name GOD UNLIMITED/UNIVERSITY OF HEALING or any variations thereof and shall not hold itself out as a CHURCH OF GOD UNLIMITED AND THE UNIVERSITY OF HEALING, it being understood that such designation is the exclusive right and privilege of GOD UNLIMITED/UNIVERSITY OF HEALING and of the AFFILIATE's duly affiliated with it.

Article IX

THE AFFILIATE AND THE MINISTER

Section 1   **VACANCY OF OFFICE.** The Office of Minister of this AFFILIATE automatically shall become vacant by resignation, death or due ecclesiastical authority relative to a minister from headquarters.

Section 2   **DUTIES OF MINISTER.** The Minister shall have and exercise all the powers,duties and prerogatives usually accorded to a Minister including, without limitation, the planning and conducting of all religious services; the planning, teaching and supervision of all classes of instruction, both accredited and nonaccredited; and the leadership, supervision and conduct of all activities of practitioners, organizations and groups within this AFFILIATE; of religious, educational, counseling, fellowship, worship activities of this AFFILIATE; conducting all special educational seminars, symposiums, lyceums, institutes, academies and training workshops teaching and demonstrating the spiritual philosophy of this AFFILIATE and its general management. The duties of the Minister as the responsible director of the AFFILIATED CHURCH, will direct its functioning, its religious life, its business life, and maintain all its affiliated operations.

Article X

AMENDMENTS

Section 1   BYLAWS. These Bylaws may be amended or repealed only by a two-thirds vote of the Board of Directors.

CERTIFICATE OF INCORPORATING OFFICER

I, the undersigned, do hereby certify that I am the incorporating officer of the

AFFILIATE: _____

and that the foregoing Bylaws consisting of ten articles, constitute the Bylaws of said AFFILIATE as duly adopted at the meeting of the Board of Directors thereof held on this

_____ day of month _____

_____ year

INCORPORATING OFFICER

Signature: _____
Print Name: _____
Address: _____
City: _____ State: _____
Zip Code: _____ Country: _____

Affiliating organization, please indicate whether you are a legal corporation or a nonincorporated group by crossing out the noneffective term. Thank you.   ∞